Coastwise Navigation

Notes for Yachtsmen

G G Watkins

STANFORD MARITIME LONDON

Stanford Maritime Limited
Member Company of the George Philip Group
12-14 Long Acre, London WC2E 9LP

First published 1962
Second Edition 1974
© 1974 G.G. Watkins

Printed in Great Britain by
C. Nicholls & Company Ltd.

ISBN 0 540 07264 8

Contents

Acknowledgements

Preface

1 An Introduction to Charts   1

2 Navigational Marks   9

3 Tides   29

4 Navigational Equipment   48

5 Compass Errors and Corrections   65

6 Laying a Course   78

7 Position Fixing   83

8 Passage Making   116

Index   121

Acknowledgements

I am indebted to the following manufacturers for the photographs of their yacht equipment:

Messrs. Henry Browne & Son Ltd, for their Sestrel compasses;

Messrs. Kelvin Hughes Division of Smiths Industries Ltd, for their chartwork instruments;

Messrs. Electronic Laboratories (Marine) Ltd, for their Seascribe echo sounder and Seafix radio D.F. set; and

Messrs. Brookes & Gatehouse Ltd, for their Heron D.F. aerial and Homer receiver.

I am obliged to the Controller of Her Majesty's Stationery Office and the Hydrographer of the Navy for permission to reproduce portions of Admiralty charts and publications including extracts from Tide Tables, and also to Messrs. Thomas Reed Publications Ltd. for permission to reproduce portions of Reed's Nautical Almanac.

G.G.W.

Preface

This book has been written with the object of introducing coastal navigation to those yachtsmen who, so far, have only sailed locally, but now wish to make coastal and short sea passages. It is hoped that it will serve also as an aid to memory to the more experienced yachtsman after his winter 'lay-up'.

The book describes the equipment required and the various factors which should be considered before leaving harbour, as well as during the passage. Wherever appropriate, simple drawings and examples have been introduced so that the text can be kept concise and clear.

The introduction by the Hydrographer of the Navy of Metric Charts, and tidal and other information in metres, for areas in United Kingdom waters has made it necessary to revise sections of the book.

This revision has also required some additions to the sections on navigational equipment and position fixing in order to cover the theoretical parts of the navigation syllabuses of the RYA National Coastal Certificates, and the RYA/DTI Yachtmasters' (Offshore) Certificate.

My thanks go to those who have assisted in any way in the preparation of this book.

G. G. Watkins
Sidcup

Chapter 1

An Introduction to Charts

Navigation is the science of finding a boat's position at sea, and of directing her safely from one place to another.

A knowledge of charts, Sailing Directions (known as "Pilots"), Light Lists, and other publications is required, as well as other aids such as buoys, lighthouses, lights, fog signals and radiobeacons.

So that these aids may be used in navigating a boat, their positions on the earth's surface must be known. It is therefore necessary to know something about the earth, and the method adopted to define position on the earth's surface, together with the units of measurement used.

THE EARTH is not a perfect sphere, but may be considered so for most practical purposes in navigation without appreciable error.

DIRECTION. The direction towards which the earth rotates is called "east". This is the cardinal point on that side of the horizon where the heavenly bodies rise. The opposite cardinal point is called "west". The end of the earth's axis of rotation which lies on the left of an observer facing east is known as the North Pole. The opposite end of the earth's axis of rotation is known as the South Pole.

POSITION. The position of any place is given by stating its latitude and longitude in degrees (°), minutes ('), and seconds ("). (There are 90 degrees in one right angle, 60 minutes make one degree, and 60 seconds make one minute).

The "latitude" of a place is its angular distance from the equator measured along its meridian of longitude from 0° to 90° north or south.

The "longitude" of a place is its angular distance from the Greenwich meridian measured along the equator from 0° to 180° east or west (see Fig. 1.1).

For example, the position of North Foreland lighthouse is:
    51 degrees 22 minutes 28 seconds north,
    1 degree 26 minutes 49 seconds east.

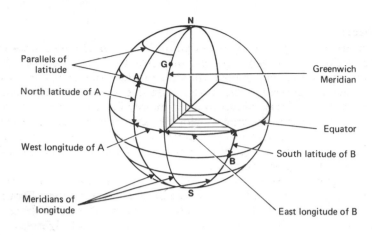

Fig. 1.1

and is written: 51° 22′ 28″ N.,
                     1° 26′ 49″ E.

Units of Distance

THE STATUTE MILE is an arbitrary unit and has no connection with any length on the earth's surface. Its length was laid down by Statute in the reign of Queen Elizabeth I as being "8 furlongs of 40 perches of 16½ feet each" giving a length of 5280 feet.

THE NAUTICAL OR SEA MILE is the unit used at sea and is approximately the distance in feet, measured along a meridian, separating two places whose latitude differs by one minute. Because the earth is not exactly spherical, this length varies from 6046 feet at the equator to 6108 feet at the poles, the mean being 6077 feet. For convenience a length of 6080 feet is used. The International nautical mile is 1852 metres.

Other Units used in Navigation

A FATHOM equals 6 feet or 2 yards.

A METRE is approximately 3.3 feet and a DECIMETRE, which is one tenth of a metre, is approximately 4 inches.

A CABLE equals one tenth part of a nautical mile or 608 feet. (Approximately 200 yards or 100 fathoms).

A KNOT is the unit of speed and is equal to one nautical mile per hour.

Charts

A chart is a map used by a navigator. The navigable sea areas of the world, and the adjacent coastlines are depicted on charts, the detail shown depending upon the scale to which the chart is drawn.

When a large area of the earth's surface is represented, the chart is a *Small Scale Chart*. These are used mainly for sea or ocean crossings to enable the navigator to plot his position and plan his route. Only the more important lighthouses and radio aids to navigation are marked upon the coastline shown, as a *Large Scale Chart* should be used when approaching the land.

A large scale chart shows a much smaller area of the earth's surface in great detail, and indicates the nature of the coastline, depths of water up to the coast, important land features visible from the sea, lighthouses and floating marks such as buoys and lightvessels, which may be used by the navigator. Information about tidal streams is shown, and also all dangers to navigation such as rocks, shoals, wrecks, etc., that must be avoided.

The natural scale of a chart is marked on it under its title, and is the ratio that a length measured on the chart bears to the corresponding length measured on the earth's surface, for example:

On a small scale chart, 1/500,000 means that one inch on the chart represents 500,000 inches or 6.85 miles on the earth's surface, i.e. 0.15in to 1 mile. On a large scale chart, 1/36,500 means one inch on the chart represents 36,500 inches or 0.5 mile on the earth's surface, i.e. 2in to 1 mile.

The Hydrographic Department of the Admiralty is the largest and most important publisher of charts in the United Kingdom. It publishes charts of all parts of the world, which are obtainable from Admiralty Chart Agents situated at more than 50 ports in the British Isles, and also at the principal ports of the world. A list of these agents is published annually in Admiralty Notice to Mariners No. 2.

To enable the necessary charts for a passage to be selected, a full catalogue of charts and publications is published by the Hydrographic Department and a copy of this may be seen at a chart agent. A Home Edition of this catalogue for the use of coastal shipping and yachtsmen is also published. It lists charts and publications relating to the British Isles and N.W. Europe from Brest to Denmark, and shows on Index charts the area covered by each individual chart.

Charts are also published by Messrs. Imray, Laurie, Norie and Wilson Ltd., and Messrs. Stanford Maritime Ltd., and these are obtainable from most chart agents and yacht chandlers. These charts are drawn with the yachtsman in mind, and they make more use of colours to present information than is done on Admiralty charts. They may often be more economical than Admiralty charts as, on a number of them, plans of ports marked on the main part of the chart are shown, drawn to a larger scale, as insets to the main chart. These plans will not show as much detail or be drawn to as large a scale as the equivalent Admiralty plan, but they are often sufficient for navigating a small vessel into port, particularly so in the case of Stanfords' charts which also print pilotage and other information on the back of the chart.

Several different projections are used by map makers in order to depict the curved surface of the earth on a flat piece of paper, and each distorts the actual area shown in one way or another. The most useful chart for a navigator is one upon which he can draw a straight line joining his starting point to his destination, and then obtain by measurement the direction in which to head his vessel. The Mercator chart, which is mathematically constructed, allows him to do this.

THE MERCATOR CHART. On a Mercator chart the equator and all parallels of latitude shown are straight lines parallel to each other. The meridians are straight lines drawn at right angles to the parallels and the equator and spaced an equal distance apart. As the meridians on the earth's surface converge towards the poles, the above method of drawing the meridians, causes distortion of land masses in an east-west direction. To preserve the correct shape of the land, the parallels of latitude, which are equally spaced on the earth, are drawn in on the chart an increasing distance apart, as the latitude increases towards the poles.

The distance between two points is measured by using the latitude scale at the sides of the chart, as one minute of latitude is equal to 1 nautical mile. Since each minute of latitude as marked on the chart gets progressively longer towards the poles, it is important that only that part of the latitude scale is used which lies abreast of the two points whose distance apart is required. The longitude scale at the top and bottom edges is never used to measure distance.

Examples of the way in which the latitude scales are divided on Admiralty charts are shown in Fig. 1.2.

THE GNOMONIC PROJECTION. Port approach and harbour charts are drawn on the gnomonic projection, as are certain special charts for ocean navigation and charts of polar regions.

On a gnomonic chart, meridians appear as straight lines converg-

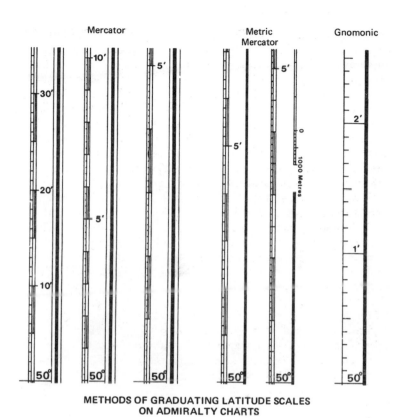

METHODS OF GRADUATING LATITUDE SCALES
ON ADMIRALTY CHARTS

Fig. 1.2

ing to the poles and parallels of latitude are curves.

On the large scale charts of small areas in the approaches to ports, etc., the curvature of the parallels, and convergence of the meridians is so slight that the chart may be used in the same manner as any other chart. Distance may be measured either by using the latitude scale as is done on the mercator chart, or from a separate scale of distance that is marked at the bottom or side of this type of chart. Large scale gnomonic charts of port approaches etc. are graduated as shown in Fig. 1.2.

METRIC CHARTS. The Hydrographer of the Navy has started a programme directed to convert Admiralty navigational charts to metric units. The first metric charts of British Isles waters were published in 1972, and it is hoped to complete the programme for this area by the end of the 1970s. The whole programme is a major task and this will necessarily mean that for many years both fathoms and metric charts will continue to be published. Metric charts are easily recognised by the greater use of colour, and by the words DEPTHS IN METRES clearly marked in magenta.

SYMBOLS AND ABREVIATIONS FROM ADMIRALTY CHART No. 5011 (BOOK EDITION)

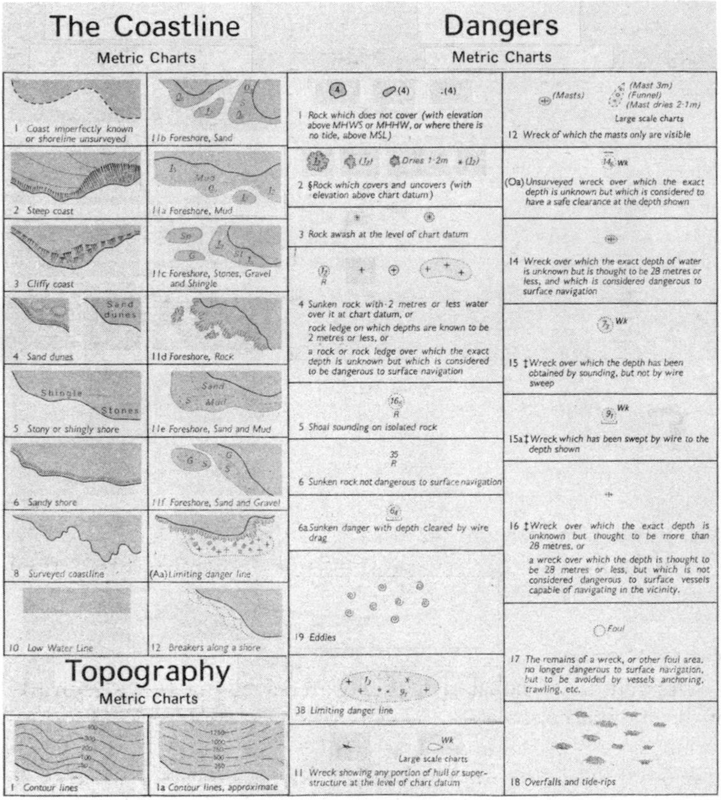

Reproduced from British Admiralty Chart No. 5011 with the permission of the Controller of H.M. Stationery Office and of the Hydrographer of the Navy.

Fig. 1.3

SYMBOLS AND ABBREVIATIONS. These are used on charts to present as much information as possible in the smallest space. Most symbols and abbreviations used on Admiralty charts are common to metric and fathoms charts, and users should have little difficulty in transferring from one type of chart to the other. They are shown on chart No. 5011, which is published in the form of a booklet, and

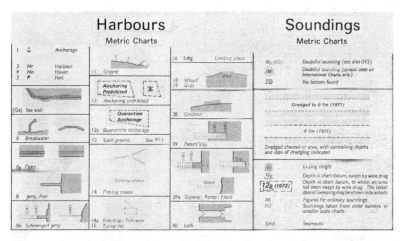

Reproduced from British Admiralty Chart No. 5011 with the permission of the Controller of H.M. Stationery Office and of the Hydrographer of the Navy.

Fig. 1.3a

are also printed in Reed's Nautical Almanac. A selection of the more important symbols and abbreviations together with their meanings is given in Fig. 1.3 and 1.3a.

Notices to Mariners

New information is constantly being received at the Admiralty about the navigable sea areas of the world. To enable this information to be passed on to the navigator so that he may keep his charts and publications up to date, the Admiralty publishes Notices to Mariners in the form of a weekly booklet, which may be seen or obtained free from Admiralty Chart Agents, Customs Houses, Harbour Authorities and Mercantile Marine Offices. Many chart agents will correct charts on payment of a fee. An example of a notice is shown in Fig. 1.4.

Number of notice, which should be put
at bottom left hand corner of chart
after information has been inserted.

***1433.   ENGLAND, E. COAST — Sheerness Middle Sand — Wreck
of S.S. Richard Montgomery — Additional Marking Buoys
laid.**

A green spherical light-buoy, *Int. Qk. Fl. G.*, *10 sec.*, with ⌇⌇ above, is to
be inserted in the following positions:

(1)   (*a*) $053\frac{1}{2}°$ 2·03 miles ⎫   from Garrison Point Radio Mast
     (*b*)   049° 1·86 miles ⎭   (51° 26′ 45″ N., 0° 44′ 46″ E. approx.).
(2)   (*a*)   1·2 cables West ⎫   of the stranded wreck in position
     (*b*)   1·0 cables East ⎭   51° 27′ 57″ N., 0° 47′ 12″ E. (approx.).

Charts [*Last correction*].—**3683 & L**(**D5**) **3683** (1) [*1432/73*]—
1185 & L(**D5**)   **1185** (1) [*1432/73*]—**1607 & L**(**D5**) **1607** (2) [*1280/73*].
Medway Ports Authority Notice 14/73.
Dover Strait Pilot 1971 p. 280.   (*H.3560/68.*)

Chart affected

Part of notice that
affects chart 1185.

Last notice affecting
chart 1185.

Decca chart affected.

Fig. 1.4

Chapter 2

Navigational Marks

Lights

The abbreviations given on chart No. 5011 to describe the lights shown from lighthouses, beacons, lightvessels and buoys, require some explanation and this is given in the following notes.

The position of a lighthouse or light beacon is indicated by a star as follows ★ or ✳ . This is further emphasised on the chart by overprinting with a magenta "splash".

A light is described by giving:
1. Its distinguishing appearance (characteristic)
2. Colour
3. Time required for one complete cycle (period)
4. Elevation ⎫ not given for light buoys.
5. Range in clear weather ⎭

1. CHARACTERISTICS used to distinguish lights, with the abbreviation given first, are as follows:

F.	Fixed. A continuous steady light.
Fl.	Flashing. A single flash at regular intervals, or a steady light with regular intervals of total darkness; in each case, the duration of LIGHT is always LESS than that of darkness.
Gp.Fl.	Group Flashing. A group of two or more flashes at regular intervals. Some lights show alternate groups with a different number of flashes, e.g. (2+3).
Occ.	Occulting. A steady light with sudden and regular intervals of darkness. Duration of LIGHT is always MORE than that of darkness.
Iso.	Isophase. Light showing equal intervals of light and darkness.
Mo.	Morse Code. Light showing long and short flashes grouped to form morse letters or numbers.

9

Gp.Occ.	Group Occulting. A steady light with a group of two or more sudden and regular intervals of darkness. At some lights alternate groups are different in number, e.g. (1+3)
F.Fl.	Fixed and Flashing. A fixed light varied at regular intervals by a single flash of relatively greater brilliance.
F.Gp.Fl.	Fixed and Group Flashing. A fixed light varied at regular intervals by a group of two or more flashes of relatively greater brilliance.
Qk.Fl.	Quick Flashing. A light which flashes continuously at sixty or more times a minute.
Int.Qk.Fl.	Interrupted Quick Flashing. A light which flashes at a rate of more than sixty times a minute, with a regular interval of total darkness.

A number, or numbers, in brackets after the abbreviations Gp.Fl., and Gp.Occ., denote the number of flashes and intervals of darkness respectively in each group. Letters or numbers in brackets following the abbreviation Mo., indicate the morse characters formed by the long and short flashes.

2. COLOUR. The abbreviations used to indicate the colour of the light exhibited are as follows: Bl. . . . Blue; G. . . . Green; Or. . . . Orange; R. . . . Red; Vi. . . . Violet; W. . . . White.

A light which has no colour abbreviation after its characteristic exhibits a white light and no other, although another separate and distinct coloured light may be shown from a different part of the same lighthouse, thus the description of the lights shown from the Skerries lighthouse off Anglesey is Gp.Fl.(2)10sec.36m.29M. & F.R.26m.16M. This indicates that groups of 2 white flashes are exhibited every 10 seconds from a height of 36 metres, and a second continuous red light is shown from a height of 26 metres in the same tower. The second light, as in the example described above, usually shows over a narrow sector in order to indicate a dangerous line of approach.

Certain lights show different colours in succession. Their characteristics are preceded by the abbreviation Alt. (meaning alternating) and followed by the colours shown. The sequence of colours indicated will be seen from any part of the visible sector covered by the light.

Wolf Rock lighthouse off Lands End shows all round the horizon in each cycle: a 0.7 sec. white flash; 14.3 secs. darkness;
a 0.7 sec. red flash; 14.3 secs. darkness.

Its description as marked on the chart for that area is Alt. Fl.W.R. 30sec.

Other lights change colour in sectors, usually to indicate either a safe approach sector, or alternatively a sector or sectors which cover some unmarked dangers, e.g. Longships lighthouse off Lands End shows a white and a red light for 5 seconds and then darkness for 5 seconds in each cycle.

The white light is shown over a 222° sector to seaward, and the red light is shown over a 19° sector northward, and a 20° sector

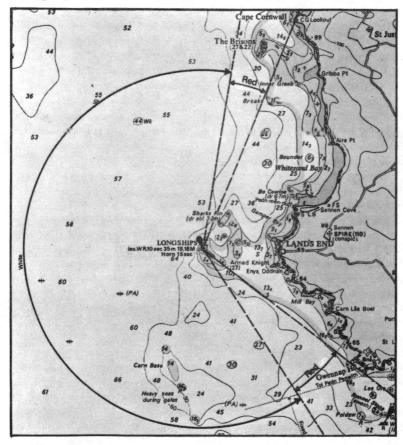

Reproduced from British Admiralty Chart No. 777 with the permission of the Controller of H.M. Stationery Office and of the Hydrographer of the Navy

Fig. 2.1 Longships Light-Sectors

southeastward, from the lighthouse as shown in Fig. 2.1. The two red sectors cover off-lying rocks and dangers off the coast. The abridged description of the light shown on the chart of this area is Iso.W.R.10sec.35m.19,18M. The sectors are only marked as shown in the figure on large scale charts. If a large scale chart is not available, reference should be made to the Light List for the area or to Reed's Nautical Almanac. It is important to note the difference between the two types of lights just described. In the case of Wolf Rock light a vessel would see both the white and red lights alternately, even if she were stopped. A vessel stopped to seaward of Longships light in the white sector would only see a white light, and she would have to MOVE into either of the red sectors in order to see the red light.

3. PERIOD. The period of a light is the time required to complete one cycle of the characteristic, i.e. from the instant when the characteristic starts to the instant when the characteristic next starts, including any intervening darkness.

For example:

Bishop Rock light shows a white light in each cycle, as follows:

flash 0.7 sec.; darkness 1.6 sec.; flash 0.7 sec.; darkness 12.0 sec.

Its period is therefore 15 seconds and its description, as marked on the chart is Gp.Fl.(2)15sec.

The Needles light shows a white, red and green light over sectors in its period of 20 seconds as follows:

light 14 sec.; darkness 2 sec.; light 2 sec.; darkness 2 sec.

The abridged description on the chart is Gp.Occ.(2)W.R.G 20sec.

It is important on first sighting a light to note its characteristic by carefully counting the number of flashes or intervals of darkness. The period should then be checked by counting or by stopwatch. If an observer starts to count at the beginning of each cycle as follows:

"and one and two and three and four and five and six etc. . . . . ."

until the cycle begins again, a good estimate of the period can be obtained (this method of counting can be practised at any time against a watch to obtain an even rate). The chart should then be examined and the light identified. When expecting to sight a light, it should not be assumed, when one is sighted, that it is the expected light until the check described above has been carried out.

4. ELEVATION. The elevation of a light given on the chart is measured in metres (or feet on fathoms charts) between the focal plane of the light and the tidal levels Mean High Water Springs

(MHWS) or Mean Higher High Water (MHHW) or, where there is no tide, Mean Sea Level (MSL). (See page 34 for MHWS).

5. THE RANGE of a light given on a chart published before 31 March 1972 is the lesser of the Geographical and Luminous ranges. All new charts and new editions published on or after the above date will give the Nominal range which is the range when the meteorological visibility is 10 sea miles, and takes account of the intensity of the light. The Geographical range assumed the observer's eye was 15 feet or 5 metres above the sea. It takes account of refraction and curvature of the earth, while Luminous range is the maximum distance the light can be seen taking into account the meteorological visibility and the intensity of the light.

When passing close to a flashing light, a faint continuous light may be seen between the flashes.

Lights are exhibited at least from sunset to sunrise and during foggy or hazy weather from before sunset to after sunrise. Lights under the jurisdiction of the Clyde Lighthouse Trust are shown during the day in fog.

Other Abbreviations used to describe Lights

"Aero". Lights marked on a chart with the word Aero placed before the characteristic are primarily for the use of aircraft, but may be visible from the sea. They are often of great luminous power and elevation, and on some coasts may be the first lights sighted when approaching the coast. These lights often have characteristics similar to ordinary navigational lights, but others flash single letter or two letter morse groups in various colours. The letter or letters shown are indicated in the characteristic marked on the chart or in the Light List; for example Aero Mo.(AB); or Aero Alt. Fl.W.G. Such lights should be used with caution as they are subject to changes which may not always be promptly notified to the mariner.

"Leading" or "Ldg" is marked against two lights which, when in line, act as leading lights in a channel or into a harbour. On large scale charts such lights will be shown as follows:

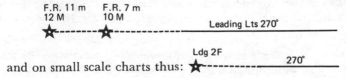

and on small scale charts thus:

Lights described as "Lts in line" are intended to mark limits of areas, alignments for anchoring, etc.; they do not mark a direction to be followed.

The full line as shown above, indicates the advised safe limit of approach to the leading lights, the dotted portion of the line being drawn to guide the eye to the lights which are to be kept in line, the figures indicating their true direction when in line. The rear light (that furthest from the vessel when on the leading line) is always placed higher than the front light, so that when in line they appear vertically one above the other.

Leading lights as seen from a boat.

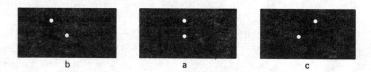

Aerial view of leads shown above.

View (a). Lights in line, boat correctly on leading line.

View (b). Front light to the right of rear light. Boat is therefore to the left of the leading line, and should steer to the right until (a) is achieved.

View (c). Front light to the left of rear light. Boat is therefore to the right of the leading line, and should steer to the left until (a) is achieved.

It will be seen from the above that if a boat is steering along the leading line, and the front light appears to move to the right, she steers to the right to regain the line. If the front light appears to move to the left, she steers to the left to regain the line. In other words she "follows" the front light or lead.

Dir.   A single leading light with a narrow sector or narrow intensified arc.

Obscd.   Light obscured in sector indicated.

Occas.   Occasional. Marked against lights that are only exhibited when a vessel is expected or at other irregular times.

Vert.   Lights placed vertically.

Hor.   Lights placed horizontally.

Fog Detr. Lt. Marked against lighthouses, which are fitted with fog detector lights, additional to the main light, for the automatic detection of fog. These lights sweep back and forth along the sea horizon, first in one direction and then in the other, exhibiting a powerful bluish flash of about one second duration. The period between flashes will vary with the position of the vessel within the arc of visibility. At the limits of the arc of visibility the duration of the flash may be considerably longer than one second. At present only a few lighthouses in the British Isles and Norway are fitted with these lights, but more will probably be fitted here and elsewhere in the future.

Lights are exhibited from structures which vary in size and construction from tall stone towers with living accommodation for keepers, down to small latticework structures built of steel angles, from which lights operate automatically. Each structure is made as conspicuous as possible against its particular background so that it may be more easily identified by day when viewed from offshore. They are often white or grey, occasionally marked with a contrasting dark band or bands, or alternatively red or black, with occasionally a contrasting white band or bands. Other colours may be used if necessary. The height of the structure may often be appreciably less than the charted elevation of the light, particularly when it is built on a cliff top. Thus Anvil Point lighthouse consists of a white tower 12m. in height but placed so that the light is exhibited from an elevation of 45m. above MHWS. Because of this, during daylight hours, a boat has to be appreciably closer to a lighthouse to identify, and make use of it, than she has to be at night when the light is exhibited.

A brief description of each lighthouse is given in the Light Lists, and "Pilot" for the particular areas involved, and in Reed's Nautical Almanac for the coasts of the British Isles, N.W. France, Belgium and Holland, and a few in Germany and Denmark.

NAVIGATIONAL MARKS

Lightvessels

These are marked on charts by the symbol , the small circle at the centre of the base indicating the exact position. The colour of the lightvessel is marked beneath the symbol as shown. Descriptions of all lightvessels, both British and foreign, are found in the relevant Light Lists and Sailing Directions.

Those situated near the coasts of the British Isles are painted red, and their names are painted in large white letters on each side. Some Continental lightvessels are red, with white vertical stripes, or white bands.

Lightvessels are placed off coasts where there are shoals extending, or lying some way off shore, and also in wide river estuaries, where the main channels lie too far from the coasts for shore lights to be of assistance, as in the Thames Estuary. Lightvessels exhibit lights with distinctive characteristics similar to those previously described, and the same abbreviations are used on charts to describe them.

A white riding light is shown forward on the forestay, 2 metres above the rail, and this when visible indicates the direction in which the lightvessel is swung, and also gives some indication of the direction of the tidal stream at that position at the time. If a strong wind is blowing this method of estimating the direction of the tidal stream should not be relied upon, as the wind may cause the lightvessel to lie across the tidal stream.

If at any time a lightvessel cannot show the characteristic light while she is on station, only the riding light on the forestay will be shown.

Other signals that may be shown from lightvessels are listed in full in the relevant Light List and in Reed's Nautical Almanac.

It should be borne in mind that lightvessels may be withdrawn for repairs without notice, and temporarily replaced by a relief vessel or light buoy exhibiting a different characteristic light.

Large Automatic Navigation Buoys (Lanby)

Some Trinity House lightvessels will be replaced over the next few years by this new type of buoy. A *Lanby* is a discus shaped steel buoy 12 metres in diameter, 2 metres deep, and fitted with a central tubular mast superstructure 12 metres high which houses the high power light. These buoys are fitted with electric fog signals having a range of approximately 3 miles, and they can be fitted with radio-beacons and racons if required. The equipment on a *Lanby* is controlled and monitored from a shore station or light tower nearby over a UHF radio link.

Wreck Marking Vessels

Wreck Marking Vessels are sometimes used instead of buoys to mark the positions of wrecks. Such vessels are painted green with the word *wreck* painted in white on each side. To indicate the side on which they are to be passed, the green shapes shown in Fig. 2.2 are exhibited from a yard by day.

Port hand	Either hand	Starboard hand

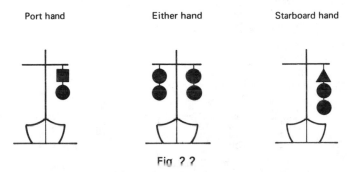

Fig 2.2

At night the shapes are replaced by green lights, and in fog two, four and three strokes, respectively, are sounded on a deep toned bell every 30 seconds. (The meanings of port and starboard hand are given on page 20).

Moveable Drilling Rigs

These may be encountered anywhere in the waters surrounding the British Isles and N.W.Europe. A rig indicates its position by exhibiting a white light flashing the morse letter U every 15 seconds visible 10 miles, and red lights flash U every 15 seconds from the extremities visible 2 miles. In fog the morse signal U is sounded by a horn every 30 seconds.

Fog Signals

During fog, many lighthouses, lightvessels and buoys, make fog signals at regular intervals. Mariners are warned that fog signals must never be relied on implicitly as sound is conveyed in a very irregular way through the atmosphere. The following points should be borne in mind. Fog signals are heard at greatly varying distances and there may be areas around a station in which the signal is inaudible. Fog may exist a short distance from a station but may not be seen from it, so that the signal may not be sounded, and some emitters cannot be started immediately signs of fog are seen. One of the tones of a fog signal which is a combination of high and low tones may be inaudible under certain atmospheric conditions. The abbreviations and descriptions of various types of signal are set out below.

Dia   A diaphone generally emits a powerful low-pitched sound which often ends with brief sound of suddenly lowered pitch which sounds like and is called the "grunt".

Siren   A compressed air siren of which there are many different types which differ considerably in their sound and power.

Reed   A reed uses compressed air and emits a weak, high pitched sound.

Explos An explosive emitter produces short reports by firing explosive charges.

Horn   Fog horns use compressed air or electricity to vibrate a diaphragm. There are a number of types which differ greatly in their sound and power. Some types, particularly those at main fog signal stations, combine simultaneously produced sounds of different pitch, to emit a very powerful signal. Others produce a single steady note, while others vary continuously in pitch.

Bell   The bell, the gong and the whistle may be operated
Gong   by machinery, sounding a regular character; by hand,
Whis   sounding somewhat irregularly; or by wave action, sounding erratically.

The obsolescent abbreviations Tyfon and E.F.Horn which may be seen on fathoms charts sound like the Horn described above, while a Nauto, short for nautophone, sounds like a Reed. Fog signals with morse or composite characteristics are shown in a similar manner to lights, e.g. Horn Mo(U); Siren(1+2).

Other Floating Marks

The edges of shoals and deep water channels in rivers and into harbours, and isolated dangers such as rocks and wrecks are usually marked by coloured buoys or floats kept in position by heavy sinkers on the sea bed. They are made of steel in distinctive shapes, and painted a distinctive colour or colours, to indicate by day what they mark, and which side they should be passed to avoid danger. Many buoys have a further distinctive shape, known as a topmark, fitted above the main structure to help identification. Most buoys are named or numbered, and these names or numbers are marked on the side of the main structure.

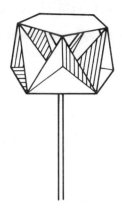
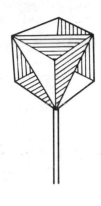

RADAR REFLECTORS

Fig. 2.3

In channels and areas used regularly by day and night, buoys and floats are fitted with automatic white or coloured lights with distinctive characteristics, to enable them to be identified and to indicate which side they should be passed. In secondary and little used channels, buoys may not be fitted with lights, and they may also be withdrawn during the winter months. To assist ships fitted with Radar, some buoys in important channels are fitted with radar reflectors, so that they show more clearly on a radar screen and at a greater range. The following symbol is marked on the chart above the position of a buoy fitted with a radar reflector ⌐⌐.

A radar reflector is shown in Fig. 2.3. It must not be confused with a buoy topmark. Topmarks are shown on pages 22 to 26.

The limitations of floating marks should be borne in mind. They may be driven from their proper positions by the action of wind, sea or tidal streams, and the boat's position should be checked by other means when possible.

A large scale chart of the area should be examined to obtain full information about a particular buoy or buoys. Some information is given in the Sailing Directions for the area, and in Reed's Nautical Almanac, but none is given in the Light Lists.

The Lateral System of buoyage has been widely adopted round the coasts of the United Kingdom, and also by some continental countries. The lateral system is used where channels are long and narrow, the buoys being placed to mark the sides of the channels.

Off some parts of the continental coastline, e.g. parts of France, where there are many off-lying rocks, reefs, and isolated dangers, buoys are placed to conform to another system known as the Cardinal System of buoyage. Where this system is used, the buoys are placed either North, East, South or West from the danger, the shape and colour of each buoy determining the direction in which the danger lies with respect to the buoy, and which side it is safe to pass.

If when navigating in a particular area, a doubt exists as to the system in use in that area, an examination of the shapes, colours etc., of the buoys marked on a large scale chart of the area will decide which system is in use and also which side to pass the buoys.

These two systems are now described in detail.

The Lateral System

In this system, the buoys are placed so that their shape, colour and light (if fitted) inform the mariner on which side he is to leave them.

In order to interpret this information correctly, it is necessary to know the direction of the *Main Stream of Flood Tide* round the British Isles. For the purpose of the buoyage system only, the fixed direction adopted by the authorities when placing their buoys, is that shown by the arrows in Fig. 2.4.

STARBOARD HAND buoys are those which must be kept on the mariner's right hand when he is entering a river, harbour or estuary from seaward; or when going *with* the main stream of flood tide.

PORT HAND buoys are those which must be kept on the mariner's left hand side in the same circumstances.

When *leaving* a river, harbour or estuary, or going *against* the main stream of flood tide, starboard hand buoys must be kept on the mariner's left hand side, and port hand buoys must be kept on the mariner's right hand side.

Thus for example if a port hand buoy is sighted off the Sussex coast from a vessel proceeding eastwards up the English Channel, the vessel is considered to be going *with* the main flood stream, and her course must be adjusted, if necessary, so that the buoy passes on the left hand side of the vessel.

If the same buoy had been sighted from a vessel proceeding *westward* down the English Channel, the vessel is considered to be going *against* the main flood stream and her course must be adjusted if necessary so that the buoy passes on the right hand side of the vessel.

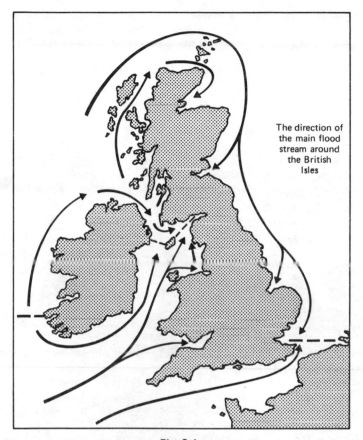

The direction of
the main flood
stream around
the British
Isles

Fig. 2.4

MIDDLE GROUND BUOYS are used to mark the ends of sand-banks or shoals which have a channel passing on each side. They indicate which of the two channels is the main channel, or alternatively that they are of equal importance. Small vessels and yachts can usually pass them on either side.

MID-CHANNEL BUOYS are used to mark the centre line or deepest part of a wide channel which also has its sides marked by port and starboard hand buoys.

ISOLATED DANGER BUOYS are used to mark an outlying shoal, rock, or danger which is surrounded by deep water.

LANDFALL BUOYS are placed to help the mariner ascertain his position when making for a channel which is situated some distance off shore, and where the land may not be easily recognisable.

WRECK BUOYS are used to mark dangerous wrecks in, or near to, frequently used channels or areas.

Details of the buoys already mentioned are given below. These buoys and their chart symbols are shown on pages 23 and 24.

STARBOARD HAND

Shape	Conical.
Colour	Black, or black and white chequers.
Topmark	(if any). Black cone point upwards, or a black diamond. The diamond is not used on a conical buoy at the entrance to a channel.

B.   B.W.   B.

Light	(if any). White, showing 1 or 3 flashes. Abbreviations; Qk.Fl.; Fl.; Gp.Fl. (3).
Remarks	If numbered, marked with odd numbers commencing from seaward.

PORT HAND

Shape	Can.
Colour	Red, or red and white chequers.
Topmark	(if any). Red can, or a red "T". The "T" is not used on a can buoy at the entrance to a channel.

R.   R.W.   R.W.

Light	(if any). Red, showing 1, 2, 3 or 4 flashes or white, showing 2 or 4 flashes. Abbreviations: Fl.R.; Gp.Fl.(2)R.; Gp.Fl.(3)R.; Gp.Fl.(4)R.; Gp.Fl.(2); Gp.Fl.(4).
Remarks	If numbered, marked with even numbers commencing from seaward.

MIDDLE GROUND

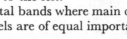

Shape   Spherical.

Colour   Black and white horizontal bands
where main channel is to the left.
Red and white horizontal bands where main channel is to
the right, or the channels are of equal importance.

Topmarks (if any):

B.W.   B.W.   B.W.

R.W.   R.W.   R.W.

R.W.   R.W.   R.W.

Main channel to the left:
Outer end: – Black cone point up
Inner end: – Black diamond

Main channel to the right:
Outer end: – Red can
Inner end: – Red "T"

Channels of equal importance:
Outer end: – Red sphere
Inner end: – Red St. George's
Cross

Light   (if any). White or Red, so that the colour and rhythm
indicate on which side the buoy should be passed in order
to keep in the main channel when entering a river or
estuary, or going with the main stream of flood tide,
i.e. Main channel to the left: as for starboard hand buoys.
Main channel to the right: as for port hand buoys.

MID-CHANNEL

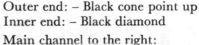
B.W.   R.W.

Shape   Usually pillar (as shown), but may
be any distinctive shape other
than conical, can or spherical.

Colour   Black and white, or red and white vertical stripes.

Topmark   (if any). Distinctive shape other than cone, can or sphere.

Light   (if any). Different from neighbouring lights on marks at
the sides of the channel.

ISOLATED DANGER

B.R.W.   B.R.W.

Shape   Spherical.

Colour   Wide black and red horizontal bands,
separated by a narrow white band.

Topmark (if any). Sphere painted black, or red, or half black and half red horizontally.

Light (if any). White or red with flashing or interrupted quick flashing character. Abbreviations: Qk.Fl.; Int.Qk.Fl.; Fl.; Fl.R.

LANDFALL AND FAIRWAY

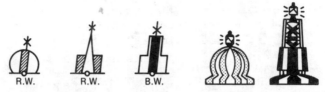

R.W.   R.W.   B.W.

Shape In accordance with rules for channel marking. Often tall pillar buoys with conical or can superstructures as shown in the figure.

Colour Black and white or red and white vertical stripes.

Light (if any). Quick flashing or flashing character. Abbreviation: Qk.Fl. or Fl.

WRECK

PORT HAND   EITHER HAND   STARBOARD HAND

G.   G.   G.

	Can	Spherical	Conical
Shape	Can	Spherical	Conical
Colour	Green, WRECK or W or ÉPAVE in white on side.	Green, WRECK or W or ÉPAVE in white on side.	Green, WRECK or W or ÉPAVE in white on side.
Topmark (if any)	Green can	Green globe	Green cone point up
Light (if any)	Green showing 2 flashes	Green occulting or green interrupted quick flashing	Green showing 3 flashes.
Abbreviation	Gp.Fl.(2)G.	Occ.G or Int.Qk. Fl.G.	Gp.Fl.(3)G.

The Cardinal System

The area surrounding a danger is divided into four quadrants named after the four cardinal directions north, east, south and west. Each quadrant is contained between the relevant intercardinal directions *from* the danger, as shown in Fig. 2.5.

Buoys are placed in one or more of such quadrants, their shape and colour indicating on which side the buoys are to be passed in order to avoid the danger.

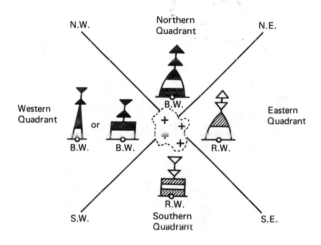

Fig. 2.5

NORTHERN QUADRANT BUOYS are to be passed on the northern side of the buoy.

Shape   Conical.
Colour   Black with wide white horizontal band.
Topmark   2 black cones, points up.
Light   (if any). White, quick flashing, flashing, group flashing, occulting or group-occulting, showing an odd number of flashes or intervals of darkness.
        Abbreviations: Qk.Fl.; Fl.; Gp.Fl.(3); Occ.; Gp.Occ.(3).

EASTERN QUADRANT BUOYS are to be passed on the eastern side of the buoy.

Shape   Conical.
Colour   Red above white divided horizontally.
Topmark   2 vertical red cones, base to base.

Light   (if any). Red, quick flashing, flashing, or occulting, showing an odd number of flashes or intervals of darkness. Abbreviations: Qk.Fl.R.; Fl.R.; Gp.Fl.(3)R.; Occ.R.; Gp.Occ.(3)R.

SOUTHERN QUADRANT BUOYS are to be passed on the southern side of the buoy.

Shape   Can.
Colour   Red, with wide white horizontal band.
Topmark   2 Red cones, points down.
Light   (if any). Red, flashing or occulting, showing an even number of flashes or intervals of darkness. Abbreviations: Gp.Fl.(2)R.; Gp.Fl.(4)R.;Gp.Occ.(2)R.; Gp.Occ.(4)R.

WESTERN QUADRANT BUOYS are to be passed on the western side of the buoy.

Shape   Can or spindle.
Colour   Black above white divided horizontally.
Topmark   2 vertical black cones point to point.
Light   (if any). White, flashing or occulting, showing an even number of flashes or intervals of darkness. Abbreviations: Gp.Fl.(2); Gp.Fl.(4).; Gp.Occ.(2).; Gp. Occ.(4).

Isolated danger buoys and fairway buoys are similar to those described in the lateral system of buoyage.

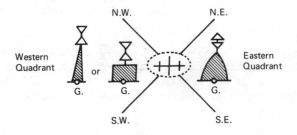

Fig. 2.6

WRECK BUOYS conforming to the cardinal system, are only placed in the eastern and western quadrants from the wreck as shown (Fig. 2.6).

EASTERN QUADRANT BUOYS are to be passed on the eastern side of the buoy.

Shape	Conical.
Colour	Green with W or ÉPAVE in white on side.
Topmark	Two green cones vertical, base to base.
Light	(if any). Green, showing groups of quick flashes, separated by intervals of darkness. Abbreviations: Int.Qk.Fl.G.

WESTERN QUADRANT BUOYS are to be passed on the western side of the buoy.

Shape	Can or spindle.
Colour	Green, with W or ÉPAVE in white on side.
Topmark	Two green cones vertical point to point.
Light	Green flashing. Abbreviation: Fl.G.

In both the lateral and cardinal systems, if buoys of the proper shape are not available, buoys of other shapes or spar buoys may be used in their places. Such buoys will be painted in a similar manner to the marks which they replace and, if lit, will show lights with similar characteristics.

Other Miscellaneous Buoys

The buoys described below are not considered as navigational buoys. They are mainly used to mark the limits of special areas wherein navigation is restricted or prohibited to ordinary vessels navigating in the vicinity. To indicate on which side they should be passed, the shapes used for such buoys generally conform to the rules for channel marking, i.e. conical, can, or spherical.

OUTFALL AND SPOIL GROUND BUOYS are used to mark the seaward end of sewage outfalls, and also areas which are used as dumping grounds by dredgers.

Colour	Yellow and black divided horizontally, or yellow and black vertical stripes.

DANGER AREA BUOYS mark the limits of any naval, military or air force practice area. Firing may take place from the shore, ships or aircraft at targets within such areas, and warning signals may or may not be shown, depending on the nature of the firing. Warning signals, when shown, usually consists of large red flags by day, and red fixed or red flashing lights at night.

Colour   (UK only) Yellow, with 2 red vertical stripes on the side, intersecting at the top of the buoy, or red and yellow chequers. Letters DZ marked in black on side.
(elsewhere) White, with 2 blue vertical stripes intersecting at the top of the buoy. Letters DA marked on side in red.

DEGAUSSING RANGE BUOYS mark the limits of degaussing ranges for testing ships degaussing equipment. Underwater cables are laid and anchoring is forbidden.
Colour   Blue and white chequers.

SUBMARINE MINING GROUND BUOYS are placed to mark the limits of practice minefields or mining grounds. Passage through these areas is usually prohibited.
Colour   Green and white horizontal stripes or green and white chequers.

MOORING BUOYS, as used for securing large vessels in, or near to, fairways. Usually they are not lit, and care must be taken in navigating in their vicinity at night.
Colour   Usually black, but any may be used.
Shape   Cylindrical or can usually.

Marking of Secondary Channels

Yachts and other small vessels often find it necessary to navigate in narrow and shallow rivers and channels in order to reach their moorings or berths. Such channels are often maintained and marked by the local harbour authority and in some cases by local yacht clubs. The buoys and marks used do not always conform to the systems previously described.

Port hand buoys are usually can or barrel shaped and starboard hand buoys usually conical, but other shapes are sometimes seen.

In some of the smaller rivers and harbours, the edges of the channel are marked by pile beacons, perches or withies driven into the mud. Pile beacons are stout poles usually with some form of distinguishing topmark. Perches and withies are tree branches also sometimes fitted with topmarks. These are rarely fitted with lights for night navigation. Reference to a large scale chart or to the "Pilot" for the area, will usually decide how to correctly pass these marks in order to keep in the channel.

Chapter 3

Tides

Tides are the periodic vertical movements of sea level in response to the tide-generating forces of the moon and sun. The solar tide-generating force is only about three-sevenths of that of the moon because of the sun's greater distance from the earth. These tide-generating forces vary as the earth changes its position relative to the moon and sun during the course of each year, thus varying the tides produced. Modern tidal theory however, suggests that the nature of the tides produced in response to the varying forces is mainly determined by the shapes, sizes and depths of the various oceans and seas, and also by the gyroscopic effect of the earth's rotation.

There are three more or less well defined types of tides and these are known as:

1. Semi-diurnal tides. 2. Diurnal tides, and 3. Mixed tides.

SEMI-DIURNAL TIDES. This type of tide is experienced at ports situated on the coasts of the British Isles and western Europe, and also in other parts of the world. At these ports sea level oscillates between high water (H.W.) and low water (L.W.) and there are two high waters and two low waters in each lunar day of about 24 hours 50 minutes. The height between successive high and low waters, called the RANGE of the tide, is only 2 metres at some ports that experience this type of tide, whilst other ports, which may be less than 100 miles away, experience tides with ranges of more than 10 metres. The semi-diurnal tides of the Gulf of St. Malo, the Bristol Channel, and the Bay of Fundy, with ranges exceeding 12 metres, have the greatest ranges of any tides experienced in the world. The main characteristic of semi-diurnal tides is that the heights of successive high waters, and successive low waters, are very nearly the same for each day. Also the time interval between successive high and low waters, called the DURATION of the tide, is approximately a quarter of one lunar day; i.e. 6 hours 12 minutes. The

29

heights of succ essive high and successive low waters do change gradually as the moon changes its phase. About $1\frac{1}{2}$ days after new moon and full moon, when the earth, moon and sun are nearly in line, the tides produced by the lunar and solar forces have the greatest range, and the highest high waters and lowest low waters are experienced. These are known as SPRING tides, and they occur every 15 days throughout the year. The interval of $1\frac{1}{2}$ days between new moon and springs and full moon and springs is because the sea does not respond instantaneously to the lunar and solar tide-generating forces. Approximately $7\frac{1}{2}$ days after new moon and full moon, the lunar and solar tide forces are acting at right angles to each other, and about $1\frac{1}{2}$ days later tides of least range are produced, with lowest high waters and highest low waters. These are known as NEAP tides, and they also occur approximately every 15 days throughout the year, on each occasion just after the first and third quarters of the moon.

Between the days of spring tides and the next neap tides, the high water heights steadily decrease, while low water heights increase. Between the days of neap tides and the next spring tides, successive high water heights increase, while low water heights decrease.

DIURNAL TIDES. Ports which experience this type of tide are situated mainly in or just out of the tropics. At these ports there is only one high water and one low water in each lunar day, and the range of tide produced is normally not large.

MIXED TIDES prevail on a large part of the Australian coast, on the Pacific coast of North America, and on the eastern shores of Asia and adjacent islands. There are two high waters and two low waters in each lunar day, but there is a marked inequality in the heights of successive high waters and successive low waters.

IMPORTANCE OF TIDES. Tides are of no importance when well offshore away from shoal areas, but in shallow rivers, port approaches and harbours, the variation of a metre or so in sea level may make the difference between staying afloat and going aground. Certain berths and anchorages can only be reached at or about high water, and on these occasions it is important to know the approximate time of high water and to what height the tide will rise. It may on the other hand, be necessary to enter a port or cross a shoal patch at about low water, and again some knowledge of the height of tide at the time will assist in choosing a safe track, or deciding whether it is safe to enter. To assist the navigator in this respect, the Admiralty publish annually in the Admiralty Tide Tables predictions of the times and heights of high and low water throughout the year at certain important ports. These predictions are published in three volumes, namely:

Volume 1. European waters (including Mediterranean Sea).
Volume 2. The Atlantic and Indian Oceans.
Volume 3. The Pacific Ocean and adjacent seas.

Each volume is divided into two parts as follows:

"Part I – Tidal predictions for Standard Ports".
"Part II – Tidal data for Secondary Ports".

STANDARD PORTS are those ports for which the times and heights of high and low water have been predicted for every day of the year.

SECONDARY PORTS are those other ports or places for which sufficient tidal information is given in the tables to enable the navigator to predict the times and heights of high and low water. This information is usually in the form of time and height differences, which when applied to the predicted times and heights of a named Standard Port, give the predicted times and heights at the Secondary Port.

All times are given for a certain meridian or zone, which is indicated on the page concerned. All heights are given in metres above CHART DATUM, except those preceded by minus signs which indicate the amount in metres that those tides are expected to fall below chart datum. (Note: At present (1973) Admiralty Tide Tables continue to give heights in feet in addition to the metric information).

CHART DATUM is the zero level for all predictions in Admiralty Tide Tables. Chart datum is a level which is fixed for each port or place after a series of tidal observations have been made there, and is a level so low that the tide will rarely fall below it. It is the datum of soundings on the latest edition of the largest scale Admiralty chart of the place. In modern practice, the datum at a place is established at or near the level of Lowest Astronomical Tide (L.A.T.) and as opportunity offers, existing older and higher datums are being gradually adjusted to approximate to L.A.T.

L.A.T. is the lowest level which can be predicted to occur under average meteorological conditions and under any combination of astronomical conditions. Such a level will not be reached every year, and it should be noted that it is not the extreme level which can be reached, as storm surges may cause lower levels to occur.

TIDES

The following extracts from the A.T.T. for European Waters will be used to show how the times of H.W. and L.W. can be obtained for a Standard Port and a Secondary Port. All times for British ports are given in British Summer Time (B.S.T.) (Zone −0100), so that from January to March and October to December when G.M.T. is being kept, one hour must be subtracted from the predicted times for these ports. All other times are given in the Standard time for the place concerned which is stated on the page for that port.

EXTRACTS FROM THE ADMIRALTY TIDE TABLES VOL. 1 FOR 1973.

(By permission of the Controller of H.M. Stationery Office and the Hydrographer of the Navy.)

CHANNEL ISLANDS—ST. HELIER

Lat. 49° 11′ N. Long. 2° 07′ W.

TIME ZONE: −0100   TIMES AND HEIGHTS OF HIGH AND LOW WATERS   YEAR 1973

	JULY								AUGUST							
	Time	M	Ft.		Time	M	Ft.		Time	M	Ft.		Time	M	Ft.
1 **Su**	0207	1·2	3·8		0218	2·1	7·0	**1** **W**	0333	0·5	1·8		0307	1·4	4·7
	0749	11·0	36·2	16	0803	9·8	32·2		0907	11·3	37·1	16	0840	10·7	35·0
	1430	1·2	4·0	M	1434	2·3	7·4		1549	0·9	3·1	Th	1520	1·6	5·3
	2008	11·3	37·2		2017	10·2	33·6		2121	11·4	37·4		2054	10·9	35·7
2 **M**	0301	0·9	2·8		0257	1·9	6·2	**2** **Th**	0413	0·8	2·7		0339	1·4	4·7
	0839	11·2	36·7	17	0836	10·0	32·9		0944	11·0	36·0	17	0910	10·8	35·3
	1521	1·1	3·6	Tu	1511	2·1	6·9		1626	1·3	4·3	F	1551	1·7	5·6
	2056	11·4	37·3		2050	10·4	34·0		2158	11·0	36·1		2125	11·0	35·6
3 **Tu**	0350	0·8	2·6		0332	1·8	5·9	**3** **F**	0448	1·3	4·4		0409	1·6	5·3
	0925	11·1	36·3	18	0907	10·1	33·2		1019	10·5	34·4	18	0940	10·7	35·1
	1608	1·2	4·0	W	1544	2·1	6·8		1659	1·9	6·1	Sa	1620	2·0	6·4
	2141	11·2	36·6		2121	10·4	34·1		2232	10·4	34·2		2156	10·6	34·9
4 **W**	0434	1·0	3·4		0404	1·9	6·1	**4** **Sa**	0519	2·0	6·7		0438	2·0	6·4
	1008	10·7	35·2	19	0937	10·1	33·3		1052	9·9	32·4	19	1012	10·4	34·2
	1650	1·6	5·3	Th	1615	2·2	7·2		1728	2·5	8·2	Su	1649	2·3	7·7
	2223	10·7	35·2		2151	10·3	33·8		2306	9·8	32·0		2230	10·2	33·6

Table 3.1

FRANCE, NORTH COAST, AND CHANNEL ISLANDS

No.	PLACE	POSITION		TIMES AT STANDARD PORT				HEIGHTS (IN METRES) AT STANDARD PORT			
	STANDARD PORT	Lat. N.	Long. E.	High Water at		Low Water at		MHWS	MHWN	MLWN	MLWS
				0900 and 2100	0300 and 1500	0200 and 1400	0900 and 2100				
1605	ST. HELIER	(see page 272)		0900 and 2100	0300 and 1500	0200 and 1400	0900 and 2100	11·1	8·1	4·1	1/3
	Alderney										
1603	Braye	49 43	2 12	+0040	+0050	+0025	+0105	−4·8	−3·4	−1·5	−0·5
	Sark										
1603a	Maseline Pier	49 26	2 21	+0015	+0005	+0005	+0010	−2·1	−1·5	−0·6	−0·3
	Guernsey										
1604	St. Peter Port	49 27	2 31	+0012	0000	−008	+0002	−2·1	−1·4	−0·6	−0·3
	Jersey										
1605	**ST. HELIER**	49 11	2 07	STANDARD PORT				See Table V			
1606	Rozel	49 14	2 02	†	†	†	†	−0·4	+0·1	−0·2	+0·3
1607	Les Ecrehou	49 17	1 56	+0012	+0004	+0010	+0020	−0·2	+0·3	−0·3	0·0
1608	Les Minquiers	48 58	2 08	0000	+0007	−0008	+0013	+0·4	+0·9	−0·1	+0·1
1609	Iles Chausey	48 52	1 49	−0012	−0016	+0004	−0002	+1·5	+1·6	+0·3	+0·2

F Tides predicted in French Tide Tables.
* In La Seine double high waters occur near Springs in the river below Duclair.
† No data.

Table 3.1a

Example. What is the afternoon time and height of low water at Braye (Alderney) on the 17 July 1973, and the time and height of the following high water?

The general index at the back of the tide tables shows a number (1603) against Braye. This indicates that it is a secondary port, and that the information for Braye will be found against No. 1603 in Part II of the tables. Standard ports are printed in the index in capitals, with the page numbers and place reference number, e.g. S. HELIER (predictions p. 272–276) . . . 1605.

On turning to No. 1603 in Part II (see Table 3.1a) it will be seen that St. Helier is the standard port, and that predictions for St. Helier are given on page 272, which is the first of 5 pages of information. On turning to the page for July the predictions are seen displayed as in Table 3.1. These times are for Zone −0100 which is the same as British Summer Time, and are as follows for PM on 17 July:

ST. HELIER

L.W. 1511 2.1 m.   H.W. 2050 10.4 m.

On returning to the page for Braye (1603) it will be seen that time differences are related to specific times of high water and low water at St. Helier, and that the height differences are related to specific heights of H.W. and L.W.

The table predicts that if L.W. at St. Helier is at 0200 or 1400, the time difference for L.W. at Braye is + 25 minutes, but if it is at 0900 or 2100, then the time difference is + 1 hour 5 minutes. If L.W. at St. Helier on the day in question comes between the times quoted, it is necessary to adjust the time difference by interpolation. Low water on the day in the example is at 1511 which comes between 1400 and 2100 and the working might be laid out as under:

Time for day	1511	Change from 1400 = 71 mins.
Reference times	1400	2100 Change 420 mins.
Time differences	+0025 —→?	+0105 Change 40 mins.

The correction to +0025 is in proportion to the change between 1400 and 1511, and 1400 and 2100, and is therefore 71/420 × 40 minutes equal to 7 minutes, which makes the time difference on the day equal to +0025 + 7 = +32 minutes.

Similarly if H.W. St. Helier on the day comes between the reference times interpolation is necessary. In this example H.W. St. Helier is at 2050, which is near enough to the reference time of 2100 to use the time difference given for that time, i.e. + 40 minutes.

The time differences to apply in this example are therefore +32 minutes for L.W. and + 40 minutes for H.W.

Height differences have to be adjusted using the same method if the heights predicted for St. Helier on the day in the example differ from the reference heights shown in Part II. In this example the position is as under for L.W.:

Height for day		2.1m.	Change from 1.3 = 0.8m.
Reference Hts.	4.1m.	1.3m.	Change 2.8m.
Ht. differences	−1.5m.	? ⟵ −0.5m.	Change 1.0m.

The correction to −0.5m. is in proportion to the change between 1.3 and 2.1, and 1.3 and 4.1, and is therefore 0.8/2.8 × 1.0m. which equals −0.3m. The corrected height difference is −0.5m. plus −0.3m. giving −0.8m.

By the same reasoning and method, the correction to apply to the −3.4m. height difference is 2.3/3.0 × 1.4m. equal to −1.1m., giving −4.5m. as the H.W. height difference.

The predicted times and heights for Braye are therefore:

St. Helier	B.S.T.	L.W.	1511	2.1m.	H.W.	2050	10.4m.
Differences			+0032	−0.8m.		+0040	−4.5m.
Braye	B.S.T.	L.W.	1543	1.3m.	H.W.	2130	5.9m.

In practice, if the predicted quantities are set down on paper as shown above, it is usually possible to estimate time and height differences by eye with sufficient accuracy for practical purposes.

The four heights given against St. Helier in Part II, i.e. 11.1m., 8.1m., 4.1m. and 1.3m. are the heights of four specific tidal levels at St. Helier.

These are MEAN HIGH WATER SPRINGS (MHWS) 11.1m.

and MEAN LOW WATER SPRINGS (MLWS)   1.3m., which are the average values of two successive high waters and two successive low waters at those periods of 24 hours (approximately once a fortnight), when the range of tide is greatest, and calculated over a year when the moon's average maximum declination is $23\frac{1}{2}°$.

MEAN HIGH WATER NEAPS (MHWN) 8.1m.

and MEAN LOW WATER NEAPS (MLWN) 4.1m., are average values calculated for similar conditions but when the range of tide is least.

The heights of these tidal levels are given for all standard ports in Table V at the front of the tide tables and in Part II as previously shown. The heights of similar levels at secondary ports are obtained by applying the height differences in Part II to the standard port heights as appropriate, e.g.

Braye MHWS: – 11.1 – 4.8 = 6.3m.
MHWN: – 8.1 – 3.4 = 4.7m.
MLWN: – 4.1 – 1.5 = 2.6m.
MLWS: – 1.3 – 0.5 = 0.8m.

The heights of MHWS, MHWN, MLWN and MLWS for selected places are also printed in tables and displayed on large scale charts. These tables also give information enabling the datum at a place to be fixed with respect to Ordnance Datum (Newlyn) the reference level of the land levelling system of the British Isles (Table 3.2).

Tidal Levels referred to Datum of Soundings

Place	Lat. N	Long. W	MHWS	MHWN	MLWN	MLWS	Datum and remarks
Sennen Cove	50° 04′	5° 42′	6·1	4·8			
Penzance	50 06	5 33	5·6	4·4	2·0	0·8	3·05m below Ordnance Datum (Newlyn)
Porthleven	50 05	5 19	5·5	4·3	2·0	0·8	2·99m below Ordnance Datum (Newlyn)
Lizard Point	49 57	5 12	5·3	4·2	1·9	0·6	2·90m below Ordnance Datum (Newlyn)
Coverack	50 01	5 05	5·3	4·2	1·9	0·6	2·90m below Ordnance Datum (Newlyn)
Helford R. Entrance	50 05	5 05	5·3	4·2	1·9	0·6	2·90m below Ordnance Datum (Newlyn)
Falmouth	50 09	5 03	5·3	4·2	1·9	0·6	2·91m below Ordnance Datum (Newlyn)

Reproduced from British Admiralty Chart No. 777 with the permission of the Controller of H.M. Stationery Office and of the Hydrographer of the Navy

Table 3.2

The information contained in such a table is often useful if tide tables are not available for making an approximate estimate of the least depth of water available at about L.W., or the maximum available at about H.W.

Tidal predictions for the British Isles and Western Europe from the Bay of Biscay to North West Germany are also contained in Reed's Nautical Almanac, but in an abbreviated form. The predicted heights and times of H.W. are given for all standard ports, but L.W. times and heights are only given for a few ports, of which London and Liverpool are examples. To obtain approximate L.W. times and heights at the other standard ports, and at secondary ports, use must be made of other information given in these tables. This consists of the average of the four spring and neap levels at the place, tabulated as Mean Level, and the average time taken for the tide to rise from L.W. to H.W. at the place, tabulated as "Duration of Mean Rise". To find the approximate height of L.W. it is assumed that the tide oscillates equally above and below Mean Level (M.L.), and that a low water height will be the same number of metres below M.L., as it is predicted the following high water will be above M.L.

TIDES

To find the approximate times and heights of low water at St. Helier on 17 July 1973 the following information for that port is

CHANNEL ISLANDS — ST. HELIER, JERSEY
Lat. 49° 11′ N. Long. 2° 07′ W

G.M.T.   Add 1 hour March 18 – October 28 for B.S.T.

HIGH WATER 1973

Day of Month	D of W	JULY Time h. min.	Ht. m.	Time h. min.	Ht. m.	D of W	AUGUST Time h. min.	Ht. m.	Time h. min.	Ht. m.	D of W	SEPTEMBER Time h. min.	Ht. m.	Time h. min.	Ht. m.
1	Su	06 49	11.0	19 08	11.3	W	08 07	11.3	20 21	11.4	Sa	08 46	10.6	20 59	10.5
2	M	07 39	11.2	19 56	11.4	Th	08 44	11.0	20 58	11.0	Su	09 15	10.1	21 29	9.8
3	Tu	08 25	11.1	20 41	11.2	F	09 19	10.5	21 32	10.4	M	09 45	9.4	22 01	9.1
4	W	09 08	10.7	21 23	10.7	Sa	09 52	9.9	22 06	9.8	Tu	10 19	8.8	22 39	8.4
5	Th	09 49	10.2	22 04	10.1	Su	10 27	9.2	22 43	9.0	W	11 06	8.1	23 40	7.7
6	F	10 30	9.5	22 46	9.5	M	11 07	8.6	23 29	8.3	Th	—	—	12 35	7.6
7	Sa	11 15	8.9	23 33	8.9	Tu	—	—	12 04	8.0	F	01 38	7.3	14 31	7.7
8	Su	—	—	12 07	8.4	W	00 39	7.7	13 31	7.8	Sa	03 14	7.8	15 42	8.4
9	M	00 31	8.4	13 13	8.1	Th	02 17	7.6	15 02	8.0	Su	04 12	8.4	16 31	9.1
10	Tu	01 42	8.1	14 26	8.2	F	03 39	8.0	16 08	8.5	M	04 55	9.2	17 11	9.7
11	W	02 56	8.1	15 32	8.4	Sa	04 38	8.5	16 58	9.1	Tu	05 31	9.8	17 47	10.3
12	Th	04 01	8.4	16 28	8.9	Su	05 24	9.1	17 41	9.7	W	06 05	10.4	18 21	10.8
13	F	04 56	8.8	17 18	9.3	M	06 03	9.7	18 18	10.2	Th	06 38	10.9	18 54	11.1
14	Sa	05 44	9.2	18 01	9.7	Tu	06 38	10.1	18 52	10.5	F	07 10	11.2	19 26	11.2
15	Su	06 25	9.5	18 41	10.0	W	07 10	10.5	19 24	10.8	Sa	07 42	11.2	19 59	11.2
16	M	07 03	9.8	19 17	10.2	Th	07 40	10.7	19 54	10.9	Su	08 15	11.1	20 33	10.9
17	Tu	07 36	10.0	19 50	10.4	F	08 10	10.8	20 25	10.9	M	08 50	10.8	21 10	10.4
18	W	08 07	10.1	20 21	10.4	Sa	08 40	10.7	20 56	10.6	Tu	09 29	10.2	21 52	9.7
19	Th	08 37	10.1	20 51	10.3	Su	09 12	10.4	21 30	10.2	W	10 15	9.4	22 47	8.8
20	F	09 07	10.1	21 22	10.1	M	09 49	10.0	22 10	9.7	Th	11 20	8.6	—	—
21	Sa	09 39	9.9	21 57	9.8	Tu	10 34	9.4	23 02	9.0	F	00 18	8.1	13 10	8.2
22	Su	10 17	9.6	22 39	9.4	W	11 36	8.7	—	—	Sa	02 18	8.3	14 51	8.7
23	M	11 05	9.2	23 33	9.0	Th	00 22	8.3	13 13	8.3	Su	03 36	9.1	15 57	9.6
24	Tu	—	—	12 08	8.8	F	02 15	8.3	14 57	8.7	M	04 31	9.9	16 49	10.4
25	W	00 48	8.6	13 33	8.7	Sa	03 43	9.0	16 09	9.5	Tu	05 18	10.6	17 34	11.0
26	Th	02 20	8.6	15 01	9.0	Su	04 46	9.9	17 06	10.4	W	05 59	11.1	18 15	11.3
27	F	03 44	9.1	16 14	9.7	M	05 37	10.6	17 54	11.1	Th	06 38	11.3	18 53	11.4
28	Sa	04 52	9.9	17 15	10.4	Tu	06 23	11.2	18 38	11.5	F	07 13	11.2	19 27	11.2
29	Su	05 49	10.6	18 09	11.0	W	07 04	11.4	19 18	11.6	Sa	07 45	11.0	19 59	10.8
30	M	06 39	11.1	18 57	11.5	Th	07 41	11.4	19 55	11.4	Su	08 15	10.6	20 29	10.3
31	Tu	07 25	11.3	19 41	11.6	F	08 15	11.1	20 28	11.0					

Day of Month	D of W	OCTOBER Time h. min.	Ht. m.	Time h. min.	Ht. m.	D of W	NOVEMBER Time h. min.	Ht. m.	Time h. min.	Ht. m.	D of W	DECEMBER Time h. min.	Ht. m.	Time h. min.	Ht. m.
1	M	08 43	10.1	20 58	9.8	Th	09 27	9.2	21 48	8.7	Sa	09 52	9.1	22 14	8.7
2	Tu	09 12	9.6	21 29	9.1	F	10 09	8.7	22 37	8.1	Su	10 36	8.7	23 04	8.4
3	W	09 45	9.0	22 06	8.5	Sa	11 09	8.1	23 52	7.7	M	11 33	8.4	—	—
4	Th	10 29	8.3	23 01	7.8	Su	—	—	12 39	7.9	Tu	00 08	8.2	12 43	8.3
5	F	11 46	7.7	—	—	M	00 22	7.8	14 00	8.2	W	01 22	8.3	13 55	8.5
6	Sa	00 49	7.4	13 46	7.7	Tu	02 34	8.3	14 59	8.7	Th	02 29	8.7	14 58	9.0
7	Su	02 32	7.7	15 01	8.3	W	03 26	9.0	15 47	9.4	F	03 28	9.4	15 55	9.6
8	M	03 32	8.4	15 51	8.9	Th	04 10	9.7	16 31	10.0	Sa	04 21	10.1	16 49	10.2

Table 3.3

TIDAL DIFFERENCES on ST. HELIER (JERSEY)
and
Depth of Water at Ports in the Channel Islands and N. Coast of France

Place	Mean H.W. *Time Diff. h. m.	Mean H.W. Height Diff. m	Mean Level m	Duration of Mean Rise h. m.	Mean Depth H.W. Sprs. m	H.W. Nps. m	Chart Datum m	Position
CHANNEL ISLANDS								
The Casquets	+0 22	−4·9	—	—	33·5	—	27·4	Anchorage S.E. of.
Alderney	+0 45	−3·8	3·9	5 53	15·5	14·2	9·1	Anchorage—rear Lt. H. open
(Braye)								Slightly Northward of front Lt. Ho.
GUERNSEY								
(St. Peter Port)	+0 06	−1·8	5·1	5 51	{ 10·8 / 18·7	8·5 / 16·5	1·8 / 9·8	Grand Havre (Anc.) / Anchorage off St. Peter Port
	See pre dictions p. 592–593							
(St. Sampson's)					7·3	4·3	Dries	Entrance to St. Sampsons.
JERSEY (St. Helier)	See pre dictions p. 586–587		6·2	5 43	13·7	11·0	2·7	Entrance and S. part of New Harbour.
Rozel	0 09	−0·15	6·1	5 47	—	—	Dries	Harbour.
Gorey	−0 05	−0·8	6·1	5 45	19·5	16·9	9·1	Outer Road (Harbour dries).
Les Ecrehoux	+0 08	0	6·1	5 40	13·9	11·4	3·0	Anchorage close to Marmotier.
Les Minquiers	+0 03	+0·6	6·5	5 48	—	—	—	
Iles Chausey	−0 14	+1·5	7·0	5 32	—	—	—	
FRANCE—NORTH COAST								
Dielette	+0 12	(−1·7Sp / −0·9Np)	5·3	5 45	4·6	2·3	−4·9	Jetty.
Carteret	+0 06	0	6·1	5 46	1·8	−0·9	−9·1	Alongside Quay
Granville	−0 15	+1·5	7·0	5 33	5·8	2·4	−7·0	Avant-port.
Cancale	−0 15	+2·0	7·6	5 30	7·5	4·3	−5·8	Head of Jétee de la

Table 3.3a

taken from Table 3.3 and 3.3a:

p.m. H.W. 1950 G.M.T. Ht. 10.4m.; Mean Level 6.2m. above chart datum; Duration of Mean Rise 5h.43m.

The time of L.W. is found by taking the Duration of mean rise from the H.W. time, i.e. 1950 − 0543 = 1407 G.M.T. and when one hour is added this becomes 1507 B.S.T.

The height of L.W. is found by calculating how much H.W. is above M.L. and subtracting this from M.L., or by subtracting the H.W. height from twice M.L., i.e.:

H.W. − M.L. = 10.4 − 6.2 = 4.2m. (This equals ½ range of tide.)

M.L. − ½ Range = 6.2 − 4.2 = 2.0m. = L.W.

or

2 × M.L. = 2 × 6.2 = 12.4m.

(2 × M.L.) − H.W. = 12.4 − 10.4 = 2.0m. = L.W.

Compared with the Admiralty Tide Table this gives L.W. 4 minutes earlier and 0.1m. lower, which for practical purposes is sufficiently accurate.

The previous example to find the times and heights of the afternoon low water, and the following high water at Braye on 17 July 1973 is now worked out using the extracts from Reed's Nautical Almanac (Table 3.3 and 3.3a).

The information required from the extracts is:

p.m. H.W. St. Helier 1950 G.M.T., height 10.4m.

Braye: H.W. time difference + 0h.45m., height difference − 3.8m.;

Mean level 3.9m.; Duration of mean rise 5h.53m.

The working can be set out as under:

St. Helier H.W.	1950 G.M.T. .... 10.4m.	
Differences	+0045 .... − 3.8m.	M.L. 3.9m.
Braye H.W.	2035 G.M.T. .... 6.6m.	2 × M.L. 7.8m.
Duration of rise	−0553	H.W. − 6.6m.
Braye L.W.	1442 G.M.T.	L.W. 1.2m.

One hour added to each of the times gives the required predictions in B.S.T.; Braye L.W. 1542 B.S.T.....1.2m.

H.W. 2135 B.S.T.....6.6m.

The results are again close enough for practical purposes to those obtained using the A.T.T.

SHALLOW WATER EFFECTS. On the English coast between Portland and Selsey Bill, on certain parts of the Netherlands coast, in the Bay of the Seine, and in most rivers and estuaries, the normal tidal pattern of semi-diurnal tides is distorted by what are known as "shallow water effects". At some ports in these areas, shallow water effects cause two high waters in succession followed by a normal low water, or two low waters in succession followed by a normal high water. These tides have what are known as double high waters or double low waters. At other ports in the same areas the tide remains at the same level for an appreciable time at high water, or at low water, and a "stand" of the tide occurs.

The tide tables predict the times and heights of both high waters or both low waters at ports where double tides occur, and also indicate at which ports there is a stand of the tide and when it occurs.

HEIGHT OF TIDE AT ANY TIME BETWEEN HIGH AND LOW WATER. The rate of rise and fall of any tide will not be uniform. Generally, at places where the tide is not distorted by shallow water effects, the rate of rise and fall is least near high and low water, and greatest near half tide or mean level.

Tables I and II are provided in the Admiralty Tide Tables to enable the navigator to calculate the approximate height of tide at any time between high and low water at standard ports. Table I gives detailed instructions and a worked example of the method of using the curves given for each standard port. Table II is a multiplication table for use in the calculations. The method can be used to calculate intermediate heights at a secondary port, but the results should be used with caution. A table is provided also in Reed's Nautical Almanac to enable intermediate heights to be calculated, and full instructions are given with it.

For use in calculating the height of tide at places between Swanage and the Nab Tower where there are considerable shallow water effects, a further special table (Table III) is provided in the Admiralty Tide Tables, and a reproduction of this table is given in Reed's Nautical Almanac. Full instructions for its use are given in each publication.

The introduction to the Admiralty Tide Tables should always be read before first using the tables, as it gives important information about how varying meteorological conditions, barometric pressure, etc., affect the tides and tidal streams, particularly in the southern North Sea.

It may not always be convenient to use the above mentioned tables. The following approximate rule may be used instead to estimate, with sufficient accuracy for most practical purposes, the height of tide at specific intervals from high or low water at places where there are no shallow water effects. There are no simple rules that can be used instead of the table for the Solent area, Table III.

The duration and range of the tide concerned should first be obtained from the tide tables. The duration should then be divided by six, and the range by twelve. Working from either high water or low water, a tide may be expected to rise or fall as appropriate for approximately:

1/12th	of its range in the first sixth of its duration;
2/12ths	,, ,, ,, second sixth ,, ,, ,,
3/12ths	,, ,, ,, third sixth ,, ,, ,,
3/12ths	,, ,, ,, fourth sixth ,, ,, ,,
2/12ths	,, ,, ,, fifth sixth ,, ,, ,,
1/12th	,, ,, ,, last sixth ,, ,, ,,

Thus using the information given for St. Helier for 17 July 1973 on page 33:

H.W.	2050 . . . . 10.4m.	1/12th range . . . . . . 0.7m.
L.W.	1511 . . . . 2.1m.	2/12ths range . . . . . . 1.4m.
Duration 0539	Range 8.3m.	3/12ths range . . . . . . 2.1m.

1/6th of duration . . . . . . 56½ minutes.

Approximate times and heights as the tide rises are predicted as follows:

L.W.	1511	2.1m.	At	1800	6.3m.
1st sixth	+0056	+0.7m.	4th sixth	+0057	+ 2.1m.
At	1607	2.8m.	At	1857	8.4m.
2nd sixth	+0057	+1.4m.	5th sixth	+0056	+ 1.4m.
At	1704	4.2m.	At	1953	9.8m.
3rd sixth	+0056	+2.1m.	6th sixth	+0057	+ 0.7m.
At	1800	6.3m.	H.W.	2050	10.5m.

The slight difference in H.W. height is caused by the "rounding off" of the increments. If heights are wanted at shorter intervals they can be obtained by graphing the above quantities, heights against times, and then lifting off heights at the required times by inspection. Such information should be used with caution.

CHARTED DEPTHS OR SOUNDINGS. The figures marked on that part of a chart which represents the sea, indicate depths of water, known as soundings, in metres, or fathoms and feet, below Chart Datum. The unit used is always stated on each chart below its title. On metric charts it is shown in addition outside the chart border in magenta. The centre of the space occupied by a sounding

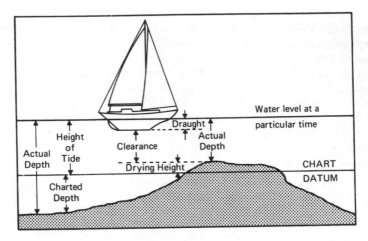

Fig. 3.1

represents the position of the depth indicated. On metric charts generally soundings are shown in metres and decimetres in depths of 20 metres or less, and in metres elsewhere.

e.g. 6_9 represents a depth of 6 metres 9 decimetres.

0_7 represents a depth of 0 metres 7 decimetres.

On fathoms charts generally soundings are shown in fathoms and feet in depths of less than 11 fathoms and in fathoms elsewhere. Some older charts show soundings in fathoms and fractions of a fathom, e.g. 7_5 represents a depth of 7 fathoms 5 feet.

0_2 represents a depth of 0 fathoms 2 feet.

$6\frac{3}{4}$ represents a depth of 6 fathoms $4\frac{1}{2}$ feet.

There will not be usually less water than the charted soundings because the tide rarely falls below Chart Datum. On the few occasions at springs when the tide does fall below Chart Datum at some places, there will be less than the charted soundings for short periods at low water.

The underlined figures, e.g. $\underline{0}_9$ or $\underline{8}$, marked on banks and rocks which uncover, express the height in metres and decimetres, on metric charts, or in feet on fathoms charts, respectively, that the bank or rock dries when the tide falls to Chart Datum.

To estimate the depth of water at any time and place, it is only necessary to add the charted depth to the height of the tide or, in the case of a bank that dries, to subtract the drying height from the predicted height of tide. This is clearly shown in Fig. 3.1.

DEPTH CONTOURS. On most charts, appropriate distinguishing lines are drawn to enclose areas which have a certain depth or less, in a similar manner to the contour lines drawn on an Ordnance Survey map. The distinguishing lines used are shown in Fig. 3.2. On many charts to emphasize the shallow water areas, a blue tint is shown between the H.W. line and the 5 metre line (or 3 fathoms on fathoms charts) and a ribbon of blue tint on the shoal side of the 10 metre line (or 6 fathoms on fathoms charts). On some charts other contour lines may be so tinted. On metric charts areas which dry are tinted green.

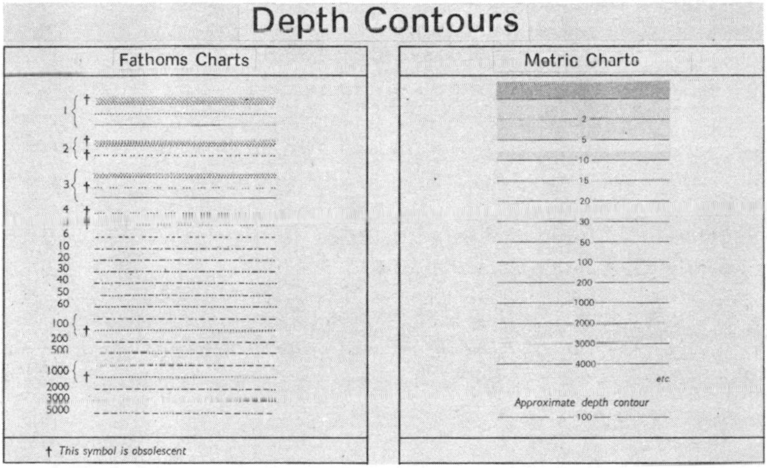

Depth Contours

Reproduced from British Admiralty Chart No. 5011 with the permission of the Controller of H.M. Stationery Office and of the Hydrographer of the Navy

Fig. 3.2

QUALITY OF THE BOTTOM. The nature of the sea bed is indicated by the abbreviations shown in the following table. This information may be of importance when looking for an anchorage with good holding ground, but too much trust should not be placed on the charted information as the sample was probably obtained by means of a lead armed with tallow which only gives an indication of the surface material.

QUALITY OF THE BOTTOM

Gd	Ground	Oy	Oysters	S	Sand	M	Mud
Oz	Ooze	Bo	Boulders	Cy	Clay	G	Gravel
Sn	Shingle	P	Pebbles	St	Stones	R	Rock
Ck	Chalk	Ms	Mussels	Sh	Shells	Cn	Cinders
Wd	Weed	f	Fine	c	Coarse	so	Soft

TIDAL STREAMS are the periodical horizontal movements of the sea in response to the tide generating forces of the moon and sun. Tidal streams react to changes in these forces, as do the tides, so that the direction and/or speed of movement of the water vary continuously throughout each lunar day and month. A tidal stream is described by stating the direction *towards* which the water is moving and by giving the speed of movement of the water, i.e. its rate, in knots. For example, a northerly stream with a rate of 2 knots means that the water is moving towards north at a speed of 2 knots. In a tidal river the tidal stream is often closely related to the rise and fall of the tide there. When the tide is rising, the stream flows into the river until at or near high water, it slackens, turns, and then flows in the reverse direction as the tide falls, until it slackens again at low water. The period when there is little or no stream is known as slack water. Nevertheless, slack water does not necessarily coincide with the times of high and low water. In rivers the stream is usually strongest in mid-stream in the straight reaches, but is usually strongest on the outside of bends. It usually pays therefore when making headway against the stream to keep near the bank in straight reaches, and on the inside of bends to avoid the main strength of the stream, bearing in mind of course that there will probably be less water available there than in midstream.

In wide channels such as the English Channel, tidal streams generally follow the trend of the channel for about 6 hours in each direction, except close to the coast where they may follow the trend of the coastline and cause indraughts into large bays and inlets. A clear indication of the set or direction of the stream is given by ships at anchor riding head on to it, or by buoys canting away from it, or by the ripple of water in the wake of buoys, piles and other fixed objects. This indication is of great assistance when berthing, anchoring or mooring, and it can save much time and labour when using the dinghy between yacht and shore.

TIDAL STREAM PREDICTIONS for specified positions are arranged in tables on most charts of coastal waters and are shown by means of arrows on the small charts contained in Admiralty Pocket Tidal Stream Atlases and Reed's Nautical Almanac. Tidal streams are also described in each "Pilot". The information given is always referred to the time of high water at a Standard Port. On charts and in the Tidal Stream Atlases, predicted directions and rates are given hourly commencing with predictions for a time which is 6 hours before H.W. at the Standard Port, and ending with predictions for a time which is 6 hours after H.W. at the Standard Port. The rates shown against each predicted direction are the Mean Spring rate which occurs on days when Spring Tides (maximum range) are experienced, and the mean Neap rate which occurs on days when Neap tides (minimum range) are experienced.

How to use the Predictions

1. THE TABLES MARKED ON CHARTS

A copy of some of the tables marked on Chart No. 1828 – England S.E. Coast, The Downs, is shown in Table 3.4.

Tidal Streams referred to H.W. at DOVER

	A 51°06'6N 1°20'4E			B 51°09'0N 1°27'8E			C 51°06'6N 1°33'3E			D 51°10'5N 1°32'2E			E 51°13'0N 1°36'4E			F 51°13'3N 1°26'6E			G 51°15'2N 1°32'6E			
Before H.W. Dover (Hours)	Dirn.	Rate (kn) Sp.	Np.	Dirn.	Rate (kn) Sp.	Np.	Dirn.	Rate (kn) Sp.	Np.	Dirn.	Rate (kn) Sp.	Np.	Dirn.	Rate (kn) Sp.	Np.	Dirn.	Rate (kn) Sp.	Np.	Dirn.	Rate (kn) Sp.	Np.	
6	224°	2·3	1·3	212°	2·2	1·2	219°	1·1	0·6	225°	1·7	1·0	190°	0·9	0·5	181°	1·6	0·9	223°	1·9	1·1	6
5	231°	2·5	1·4	213°	2·2	1·2	227°	2·5	1·4	225°	2·5	1·4	191°	2·3	1·3	183°	2·1	1·1	228°	2·5	1·4	5
4	233°	2·4	1·3	216°	1·9	1·1	225°	3·6	2·0	222°	3·1	1·7	195°	3·1	1·7	186°	2·1	1·2	226°	3·1	1·7	4
3	225°	1·5	0·8	228°	1·3	0·8	224°	3·2	1·8	219°	2·9	1·6	196°	3·2	1·8	188°	1·9	1·0	225°	3·1	1·7	3
2	075°	0·3	0·2	Slack			220°	1·8	1·0	224°	1·4	0·8	195°	2·0	1·1	190°	0·8	0·5	231°	1·2	0·7	2
1	056°	2·3	1·3	032°	1·2	0·7	050°	0·4	0·2	014°	0·5	0·3	Slack			007°	0·9	0·5	040°	1·3	0·7	1
H.W.	063°	3·9	2·2	038°	2·0	1·2	043°	2·1	1·8	040°	2·2	1·2	013°	1·3	0·7	001°	2·1	1·2	041°	2·7	1·5	H.W.
Hours	Dirn.	Sp.	Np.	Dirn.	Sp.	Np.	Dirn.	Sp.	Np.	Dirn.	Sp.	Np.	Dirn.	Sp.	Np.	Dirn.	Sp.	Np.	Dirn.	Sp.	Np.	Hours
1	064°	4·1	2·3	039°	2·3	1·3	046°	3·0	1·6	042°	3·0	1·7	015°	2·4	1·4	001°	2·3	1·3	043°	2·8	1·6	1
2	066°	2·5	1·4	031°	1·5	0·8	046°	2·4	1·3	037°	3·0	1·6	016°	2·8	1·6	002°	2·0	1·1	046°	2·4	1·3	2
3	072°	2·6	1·4	Slack			038°	0·9	0·5	047°	1·9	1·1	017°	2·6	1·5	002°	1·4	0·8	049°	1·7	1·0	3
4	087°	1·3	0·7	203°	1·0	0·6	Slack			061°	0·9	0·5	018°	1·7	1·0	017°	0·6	0·3	055°	0·7	0·4	4
5	208°	1·1	0·6	203°	1·0	0·6	Slack			167°	0·3	0·2	018°	0·6	0·3	161°	0·3	0·2	171°	0·2	0·1	5
6	220°	2·2	1·2	210°	1·8	1·0	210°	0·8	0·4	218°	1·3	0·7	189°	0·5	0·3	180°	1·3	0·7	219°	1·5	0·9	6

(right-hand column heading: After H.W. Dover, Hours)

Table 3.4

Each table shows the predicted tidal streams at the position given. Each position is identified on the chart by marking it with the appropriate lettered symbol Ⓐ or Ⓑ or Ⓒ etc., which is also marked at the head of the table to which it refers. The left hand column shows that the standard port is Dover, and shows the hours before and after H.W. at Dover for which the predictions are given. The tidal stream directions are given in degrees, where 000° indicates North, 090° – East, 180° – South, 270° – West. Spring rates are shown in the column headed Sp. and neap rates in the column headed Np., and are given in knots. The directions are always given as true directions.

ENGLAND, SOUTH COAST—DOVER

Lat. 51° 07' N. Long. 1° 19' E.

TIME ZONE: −0100   TIMES AND HEIGHTS OF HIGH AND LOW WATERS   YEAR 1973

APRIL Time	M	Ft.	Time	M	Ft.	MAY Time	M	Ft.	Time	M	Ft.	JUNE Time	M	Ft.	Time	M	Ft.
0539	1·2	3·9	0626	0·8	2·5	0541	0·9	3·0	0635	1·1	3·5	0653	0·7	2·4	0010	5·9	19·5
1 1037	6·0	19·6	16 1124	6·2	20·4	1 1038	6·2	20·5	16 1135	6·1	19·9	1 1145	6·5	21·4	16 0722	1·3	4·3
Su 1802	1·1	3·7	M 1845	0·9	3·1	Tu 1805	0·9	3·0	W 1854	1·1	3·7	F 1918	0·7	2·2	Sa 1227	6·1	20·1
2256	6·3	20·6	2338	6·4	21·1	2257	6·6	21·5	2351	6·2	20·2				1942	1·2	4·0
0622	0·9	2·9	0706	0·8	2·5	0628	0·7	2·1	0711	1·1	3·6	0006	6·6	21·7	0044	6·0	19·8
2 1113	6·3	20·6	17 1159	6·3	20·8	2 1120	6·5	21·2	17 1209	6·2	21·2	2 0746	0·6	2·1	17 0759	1·3	4·2
M 1841	0·9	2·9	Tu 1922	0·9	3·0	W 1850	0·7	2·3	Th 1929	1·1	3·6	Sa 1232	6·6	21·6	Su 1300	6·2	20·4
2331	6·6	21·6				2339	6·7	22·1				2011	0·5	1·8	2017	1·2	3·9

Table 3.5

43

Example: Assume that the direction and rate of the stream is required off Dover at 1300 British Summer Time on May 16 1973. The time and height of the nearest H.W. at Dover is first taken from the Tide Tables (see Table 3.5).

The nearest time shown is 1135 B.S.T. and the height is 6.1 metres above chart datum. The height of the next low water after 1300 is 1.1 metres, so that the range of that particular tide is 6.1 − 1.1 equal to 5.0 metres. The time of H.W. Dover is now compared with the time for which information is required, and the interval from H.W. found. In this example 1300 is 1 hour 25 minutes after H.W. at Dover. If the chart (Fig. 3.3) is now examined in the vicinity of Dover Harbour, the symbol ⬦ will be seen, indicating that predictions for that position are given in table A. On looking at table A, it will be seen that predictions for intervals after H.W. Dover are in the lower half of the table, and that for 1 hour after H.W. the direction and rates given are 064°, 4.1 knots at Springs, 2.3 knots at Neaps. For 2 hours after H.W. predictions are 066°, 3.5 knots at Springs, 1.9 knots at Neaps.

The interval for which predictions are required is approximately half way between those given above, so that by averaging these predictions, the required direction and rates obtained are 065°, 3.8 knots at Springs, 2.1 knots at Neaps.

The rate for the day in question is found by comparing the range of the tide on that day, with the spring or neap range as appropriate, taken from Table 3.6 marked on the chart, or found in the tide tables.

At Dover the spring range is 21.9 − 2.5 which gives 19.4 feet or 5.9 metres. (Use conversion table on chart, in tide tables, or Reed's Almanac). The neap range is 17.5 − 6.5 which gives 11.0 feet or 3.4 metres. If the range on the day had been nearly 5.9 metres (Springs) the rate would have been taken as 3.8 knots; if nearly 3.4 metres (Neaps) the rate would have been taken as 2.1 knots.

The rate for a day other than at Springs or Neaps is found by

Tidal Information and Chart Datum

| Place | Height above datum of soundings | | | | Datum to which soundings are reduced and Remarks |
| | High Water | | Low Water | | |
	Mean Springs	Mean Neaps	Mean Springs	Mean Neaps	
Margate	15·4 feet	13·0 feet	1·9 feet	4·5 feet	8·20 ft. below Ordnance Datum (Newlyn)
Ramsgate	16·2 ,,	12·6 ,,	1·4 ,,	4·1 ,,	8·46 ft. below Ordnance Datum (Newlyn)
Deal	20·1 ,,	16·3 ,,	2·5 ,,	6·7 ,,	11·17 ft. below Ordnance Datum (Newlyn)
Dover	21·9 ,,	17·5 ,,	2·5 ,,	6·5 ,,	12·03 ft. below Ordnance Datum (Newlyn)

Reproduced from British Admiralty Chart No. 1828 with the permission of the Controller of H.M. Stationery Office and of the Hydrographer of the Navy.

Table 3.6

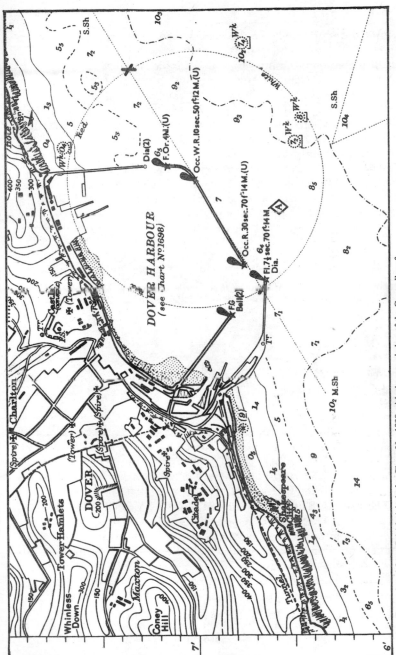

Fig. 3.3

Reproduced from British Admiralty Chart No. 1828 with the permission of the Controller of H.M. Stationery Office and of the Hydrographer of the Navy.

45

dividing the actual range on the day by the Spring range and multiplying the answer by the Spring rate of stream.

In this example, the information available is:

Spring range from chart 5.9 metres: actual range 16 May 5.0 metres; Spring rate 3.8 knots.

Therefore the rate required is 5.0/5.9 × 3.8 knots, which equals 3.2 knots. The predicted direction and rate of the stream off Dover at 1300 on 16 May 1973 is therefore 065°T. at 3.2 knots.

Note: As previously mentioned, slack water does not necessarily coincide with the time of H.W. or L.W. at a place. Although position A on chart 1828 is less than one mile from Dover Harbour, it can be seen from Table A, that when it is H.W. there, the stream is setting at 3.9 knots at springs and 2.2 knots at neaps.

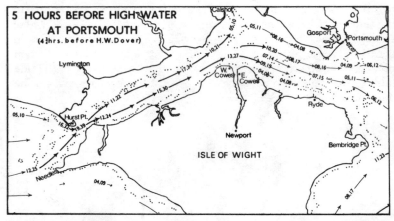

Reproduced from British Admiralty Pocket Tidal Stream Atlas (N.P. 337) with the permission of the Controller of H.M. Stationery Office and of the Hydrographer of the Navy.

Fig. 3.4

2. THE TIDAL STREAM ATLASES AND REED'S NAUTICAL ALMANAC.

The Admiralty publish eleven pocket atlases, which between them cover most of the coastline of the British Isles. Reproductions of many of these, to a smaller scale, are contained in Reed's Nautical Almanac.

A part of one of the charts contained in the Atlas for The Solent and Adjacent Waters is reproduced in Fig. 3.4. Each atlas contains thirteen small charts, with the information displayed in a similar manner. Each chart shows the directions and rates of the streams in all parts of the area at the time marked upon it. The directions of the streams are indicated by arrows. If the direction is required at a particular position in degrees, it can be estimated by eye, or found by drawing a meridian from top to bottom of the chart through the position, and measuring the angle between it and the nearest arrow. Rates are marked close to the arrow for which the information is given in tenths of a knot for neaps and springs.

For example 5 hours before H.W. at Portsmouth, the stream off Hurst Point is marked as follows: 19.39. This indicates a neap rate of 1.9 knots, and a spring rate of 3.9 knots, at that position, and the direction is approximately 060°. The actual rate on the day concerned is found in a similar manner to that described for the tables on charts, or by using the simple graph at the front of the atlas. The times for which the predictions are given are found by adding or subtracting the relevant time intervals marked on the charts to the times of H.W. at the standard port on the day in question. These times, for one or more days if necessary, can then be marked in pencil on their appropriate charts, so that the atlas can be used when planning or making a passage without constantly referring to the tide tables. If an atlas is to be used on a passage, this preparation can be done before the boat leaves port.

Chapter 4

Navigational Equipment

Many of the aids used when navigating in narrow channels and estuaries have been described. Sufficient has probably already been written to enable a person with good eyesight and suitable charts to navigate in these areas in good visibility by working from buoy to buoy, identifying each in turn and then looking ahead for the next.

In these areas in poor visibility, and when longer coastal and sea passages are to be made, certain instruments and equipment will be required to allow the boat's position to be plotted on the chart, and to enable her to be steered from place to place. These will now be described.

CHART TABLE. A flat board should be provided to act as a chart table, with minimum dimensions 22in athwartships by 30in fore and aft, but larger if possible. This can be made of ¼in or ⅜in ply, braced and stiffened so that it does not warp, and either portable so that it can be stowed in port, or hinged at the boat's side so that it can be folded up when not in use. There is no fixed size for Admiralty Charts when open, but all when folded will fit into a space 20in × 28in. If the table is made in the form of a box to the above minimum size, and 1 in or so deep, the space beneath the table can be used for stowing charts not in use. The table should be securely fixed when in use, and if possible a small seat should be arranged opposite to it, so that the navigator can get his knees under the table and brace himself against the boat's movement. If night passages are to be made, a light will be required over the table. Stowage in racks should be arranged near the table for a parallel ruler, pencils, dividers, rubbers, and the various publications which have to be used.

PARALLEL RULERS are made of perspex, boxwood or brass, and are either bar type or roller type. A suitable rule for a small chart table would be 15in long. An index is marked at the middle of one edge, and the other edge and the two ends are graduated in degrees

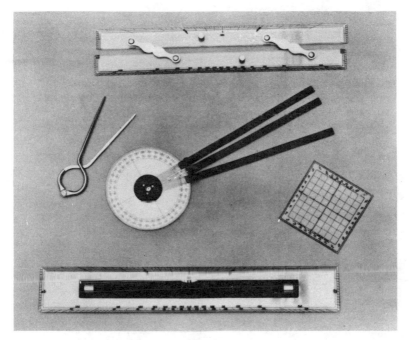

Fig. 4.1

anticlockwise from 000° to 179°, with secondary marking from 180° to 359°. A parallel ruler is used for drawing, or "laying off" on the chart courses and bearings, or for measuring courses. Its method of use will be described later.

THE "DOUGLAS" COMBINED PROTRACTOR AND PARALLEL RULE is made from transparent celluloid in two sizes, 5in square and 10in square. As can be seen in Fig. 4.1 it is a square protractor, graduated from 000° to 359° both clockwise and anti-clockwise. Pencil lines may be drawn on its underside which has a matt surface. It can be used instead of a parallel ruler for laying off, or reading off courses and bearings, and instructions for its use are supplied with it. It is less likely to be damaged than a parallel ruler, and is cheaper.

DIVIDERS are required for measuring distances on a chart. Those most suitable are made of brass with steel points, and should be at least 4in long. A pair of drawing compasses is also useful for marking in the ranges of various lights and for plotting position circles.

PENCILS AND RUBBERS. More than one pencil should be carried, preferably B grade and hexagonal, and two or three small soft rubbers.

LOGBOOK. A stiff covered exercise book can be used as a logbook for recording courses steered, positions, weather, and any important events which occur. A small pad or notebook for noting bearings and other readings should also be carried.

THE MAGNETIC COMPASS indicates the direction of compass north and when suitably graduated other directions relative to compass north can be obtained. It consists of a graduated or marked mica compass "card" secured to a hemispherical float to which are attached two parallel tubular cases containing magnetised needles, or a ring magnet magnetised along one diameter. The centre of the float rests on a hardened pin centred at the bottom of a bowl filled with a mixture of ethyl alcohol and distilled water. A wire or painted lubber line inside the bowl indicates the direction in which the boat is heading. There is a filling plug on one side to allow the bowl to be topped up when necessary. The bowl is supported in gimbals in a brass binnacle so that it always remains horizontal. (See page 52). Two diametrically opposite marks are engraved on the outside of the binnacle so that it can be lined up correctly in the boat. A hood is often fitted to protect the card from sunlight, and some form of lighting is usually provided.

Many compasses are gimballed internally and filled with a low drag spirit to damp the card's movement. The bowl may be suspended from a bracket instead of being fitted in a binnacle.

GRADUATION OF COMPASS CARDS. Compasses sold specifically for use in yachts usually have their cards graduated every 2°, or alternatively every 5° for clarity. They can be manufactured in black with white markings, or white with black markings. Many are also marked with the cardinal and inter-cardinal headings N., N.E., E., S.E., etc., and a few may still be met marked in points and half and/or quarter points (Fig. 4.2). The three possible methods are described below in the order in which they are likely to be met.
The Three Figure Method. When using this method a direction is always described in terms of three figures, and the card is graduated in degrees clockwise from 000° (N.) through 090° (E.), 180° (S.) and 270° (W.) to 359°. The direction S.E., for example, would be described 135°. This is the simplest and most accurate method of describing a direction, and its use is recommended.

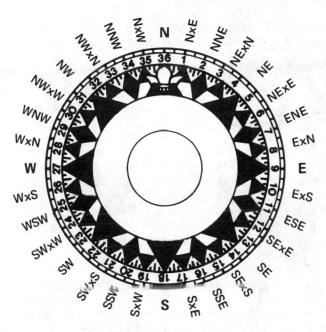

Fig. 4.2 Compass card graduated in points and quarter points, and every 5°; in the 'three figure' notation, the last 0 at each ten degree mark being omitted to allow larger figures to be used

The Quadrantal Method. This method uses the cardinal points and degrees to describe a direction. The four quadrants of the card are each divided into 90 degrees, with zero at N. and S., and 90 at E. and W. The four cardinal directions are described simply as N., E., S. or W., while intermediate directions are named from N. or S. towards E. or W. The direction S.E. for example, would be described S.45°E.

The Point Method. Because the complete card contains 4 right angles or 360 degrees, and is divided into 32 points, one "point" is $11\frac{1}{4}°$. On many cards, each point is further divided into "halfpoints" ($5\frac{5}{8}°$), and "quarter points" ($2\frac{13}{16}°$). A conversion table is contained in Reed's Nautical Almanac, enabling a course given in degrees to be changed into points and quarter points, or vice versa. Some hand bearing compasses are marked in quarter points as well as degrees.

Compass Types

STEERING COMPASSES. A steering compass is required and must be placed in the boat so that the card and lubber line can be

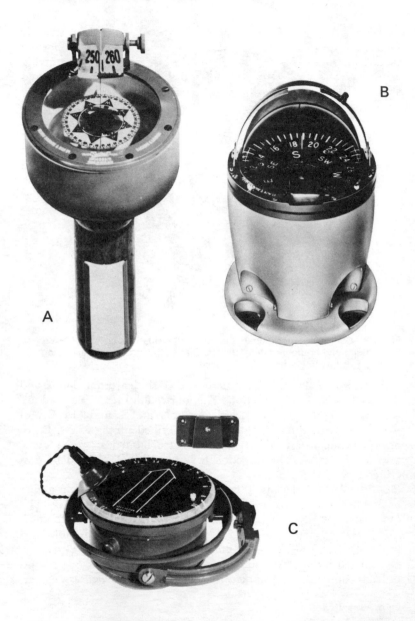

Fig. 4.3 A selection of compasses. A. Hand Bearing Compass
B. Major Compass, and C. Grid Compass (Henry Browne & Son Ltd.)

seen clearly by the helmsman. In boats fitted with wheel steering this is fairly easily achieved by placing a compass with a normal card, on a pedestal or bracket forward of the wheel. A magnifying prism or glass can sometimes be fitted to enlarge the lubber line and adjacent portion of the card.

Some cards are graduated at every second degree, and others at every fifth degree, to make the graduations clearer. In a yacht steered by a tiller, the helmsman will have to move from side to side, and may not be able to see clearly the card of a compass placed over the boat's keel. The proper course may not be steered when the compass is viewed from one side because of parallax. With tiller steering, a grid type steering compass placed under the tiller is often more convenient and easier to steer by. There are two types of grid compass, but both are used in the same manner. One type has a normal compass card, with the addition of a red wire attached to the top of the card and passing through the N. and S. points.

The lubber line runs across the diameter of the bowl, beneath the glass. A rotatable grid ring graduated from 0° to 359° with a parallel

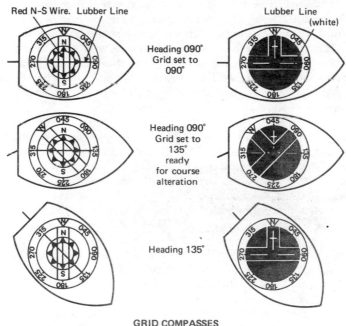

GRID COMPASSES

Fig. 4.4

wire on each side of the 0° – 180° direction, is fitted on top of the compass bowl. (See Fig. 4.4). To point or head the boat in a particular direction, the following method is used. Assuming for example, that the boat is to be headed 135° (S.E.), the grid ring is first rotated until the 135° graduation on the ring is in line with the forward end of the lubber line, and is then clamped to the bowl. The boat is then turned until the grid wires lie parallel to, and each side of, the red N. – S. wire on the card with the N. mark on the grid ring immediately over the N. end of the red wire. The boat will then be heading 135° (S.E.), and can easily be kept heading in that direction by keeping the grid wires parallel to the red wire on the card, even when the compass is viewed from one side. The other type of grid compass was primarily designed for use in aircraft, but a large number of these have been sold to the public as surplus Government stores. The card is black, and is marked with two white lines in the E. – W. direction, and at right angles to these a further white line to indicate the direction of N. The grid ring is graduated in degrees from 000° to 359°, and white grid wires are fitted to it in the form of an inverted "T" as shown. The boat is headed in the required direction by turning and clamping the grid ring as before, and then turning the boat until the grid wires lie each side of the white lines on the card. *Note:* When turning a boat so that she heads in a particular direction, it must always be remembered that the boat, and hence the compass bowl and lubber line turn round the card. The compass card does *not* move, beyond adjusting itself for deviation, although it will appear to move.

THE HAND BEARING COMPASS. In most small yachts, it is not possible to place the steering compass in a position suitable for taking the bearings required to fix the boat's position. It is therefore usual to carry a separate hand bearing compass for this purpose. A hand bearing compass is shown in Fig. 4.3. To take a bearing, the prism is first adjusted so that when looking horizontally at it across the bowl, a reflected image is seen of the card and a line engraved on the top of the bowl. The object, the notch at the top of the prism, and the image of the engraved line, are now brought into line, and the direction noted in the prism where the engraved line cuts the card. This direction in degrees is the required bearing of the object. The hand bearing compass should at all times be kept at least 4 feet away from the steering compass, and when taking bearings well clear of any steel or iron fittings such as backstays etc.

THE PATENT LOG is used for measuring the distance sailed through the water. It consists of a rotator attached to one end of a special braided line the other end of which is connected to a register which records the distance. The register fits into a shoe secured to the boat's transom, and the rotator is towed astern by the line. Each mile sailed through the water is registered after the rotator has made a fixed number of revolutions as it is towed through the water. The length of line required for accurate registration of distance depends upon the height of the register above the sea and the maximum speed of the boat. (Fig. 4.5).

Messrs. Thomas Walker & Son Ltd. make two types suitable for small craft, the Excelsior IV Log and the Knotmaster Log. Recommended lengths for the line are supplied by them with each log. A sinker is supplied with each of these logs to keep the rotator immersed in the water. These patent logs register distance sailed through the water accurately at speeds above 2–2½ knots in fine weather, but will tend to under-register at speeds below 2 knots, and when running before a heavy sea. They will tend to over-register in strong winds from ahead or on the bow.

In motor yachts the log is best streamed alongside from a suitable bracket, or a longer than normal length of line should be used to keep the rotator out of the broken water in the wake. To take in or hand the log, first unhook the line from the register and then pay out this end of the line over the transom while the rotator is hauled in, to avoid getting turns in the line. Once the rotator is inboard, the line now trailing astern can be hauled in and coiled down free of turns.

The register of a towed log can be fitted with a generator. The varying current generated can then be applied to a properly calibrated meter to indicate speed through the water.

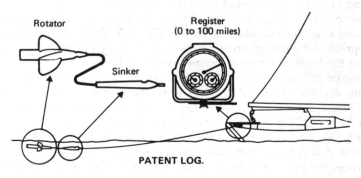

PATENT LOG.

Fig. 4.5

PRESSURE LOGS measure speed through the water, and in some logs the speed information can be integrated to provide distance through the water. One type consists of two vertical tubes, side by side, both open at their lower ends, and immersed in the sea below the hull. One tube has its open end pointing forward, and both open ends are at the same pressure when the boat is stopped. When making way through the water the pressure in the forward facing tube is increased and the difference in pressure between the two tubes operates a meter calibrated to indicate speed. Another type has a spring loaded needle inserted through a fitting in the bottom of the boat. When stopped the needle is vertical, but when the boat is moving through the water, the pressure applied to the needle "hinges" it through an arc towards the stern. This motion is proportional to the boat's speed, and the instrument's output is applied to speed and distance meters.

IMPELLER LOGS consist of a screw-type impeller mounted at the tip of a streamlined fin projecting about 3in through a hull fitting in the bottom of the boat. This fitting usually includes a valve to enable the unit to be withdrawn for maintenance or to prevent damage on grounding. A weed deflector is fitted in line with the impeller.

The impeller contains a magnet and as this is rotated by the boat's forward motion, the rotating field of the magnet induces small pulses of current in a coil contained in the underwater unit. These pulses are fed by screened cable to an electronic counter which produces a record of distance sailed each one hundredth of a mile after a fixed and designed number of pulses, e.g. Brookes and Gatehouse Ltd. "Harrier" log, 256 revs. of impeller for one hundredth of a mile. The rate of arrival at the instrument of the pulses from the impeller is measured, converted to a proportional current and applied to a speed meter. Other designs use a small paddle wheel instead of an impeller to produce the same result, with, it is claimed, less fouling by weed. In another design a non-retractable impeller is linked to the speed and distance meter by a cable which transmits the impeller's revolutions directly to the meter in the same way as does the log line in the towed log. (Fig. 4.6).

It is important to try to site the impeller clear of turbulent water. For sailing yachts and displacement power boat hulls, a position about one third of waterline length from the forward end of the waterline, and 300mm (12in) away from the centre line has often been found to be satisfactory. Sailing yachts may require an im-

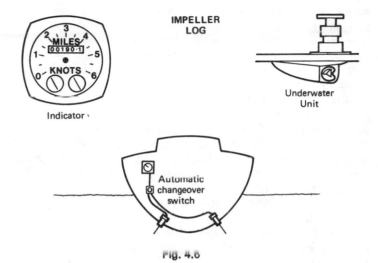

Fig. 4.6

peller on each side for best results with a gravity operated switch selecting the signals from the lee side unit automatically. High speed power boats may need the impeller fitted one quarter of length from aft, and the mechanical log may also have to be sited in the after part of the yacht.

This type of instrument once calibrated and adjusted should measure speed through the water within about ± 5% of speed from 0.7 knot upwards, and distance within ± 2% of distance run through the water.

CALIBRATION. All logs measure distance and/or speed through the water. They require calibration and this can be done by making two runs in opposite directions over a measured distance when the tidal stream is negligible or constant. The percentage log error is given by the expression $100 \left\{ \dfrac{V_1 + V_2}{L_1 + L_2} - 1 \right\}$ where:

V_1 and V_2 are the actual observed speeds over the ground for each run, and L_1 and L_2 are the speeds indicated by the log for each run. This error is not necessarily constant over the whole range of boat speeds, and if possible should be checked at other speeds. The error can be used to apply a correction to any reading obtained, or used to adjust the instrument by means of a calibration control provided by the manufacturers until the error is negligible.

THE DUTCHMAN'S LOG can be used to estimate the boat's speed when it is so low that the patent log is inaccurate. The speed can be found by calculation, by observing the time taken for the boat to pass a floating and stationary object close alongside. This can be done by throwing some small buoyant object ahead and to one side of the boat, and then noting the times when first the stem, and then the transom, pass the object. If a table has been previously worked out, based on the boat's overall length, the speed can be obtained by inspection from the table by entering it with the time interval observed. To draw up such a table, multiply the overall length of the boat (in feet) by 3600 (the number of seconds in 1 hour), and divide the answer by 6080 (feet in 1 sea mile). The answer gives the speed in knots appropriate to a time interval of 1 second. By dividing this figure in turn by 2, 3, 4, 5, etc., the speed appropriate for each of these time intervals (in seconds) can be obtained, and then drawn up in a table.

Example. For a boat with overall length of 20 feet.

$$\text{Speed for a time interval of 1 sec.} = \frac{20 \times 3600}{6080}$$
$$= 11.8 \text{ knots.}$$

DUTCHMAN'S LOG TABLE

Interval (Secs.)	Speed (Knots)	Interval (Secs.)	Speed (Knots)
2	5.9	6	2.0
3	3.9	7	1.7
4	3.0	8	1.5
5	2.4	9	1.3
		and so on	

SOUNDING. The simplest method of taking quick soundings in shallow water is to use a long boat hook or a long bamboo cane weighted at one end. These can be marked in feet by painting alternate foot lengths with black or white paint. Boats sailing frequently in shallow creeks and rivers often carry such a sounding pole secured in the rigging ready for instant use.

A Boat's Lead and Line should be carried for sounding in less shallow water. It consists of a 7lb lead or weight secured to the end of a 14 fathoms length of 2½lb line (about ⅞in circ.). The line should have a long eye spliced in one end and should then be wetted and stretched. It should then be marked from the end of the eye splice by tucking the following material through the strands of the line:

At 1 fathom, 2 fathoms and 3 fathoms respectively – 1, 2 and 3 strips of leather.

At   5 fathoms   –   A piece of white duck.

At   7 fathoms   –   A piece of red bunting.

At 10 fathoms   –   A piece of leather with a hole in it.

At 13 fathoms   –   A piece of blue serge.

Each of the first 3 fathoms is further marked in feet by pieces of cord with 1, 2, 3, 4, and 5 knots respectively.

The line is bent to the lead by passing the eye splice through the becket on the lead, and then passing the lead through the eye and pulling tight. When a sounding is required with the boat underway, the lead is hove ahead of the boat from the weather side, and the sounding read off when the line is up and down with the lead on the bottom. When sounding in deep water the boat may have to be hove to for a short time while the sounding is obtained. The line is best kept on a small reel when not in use.

ECHO SOUNDERS suitable for use in yachts can be obtained. They can be designed to work from internal batteries or from the boat's main supply of 12 to 36 volts.

A yacht installation consists of the depth indicator, a rotating neon bulb within a scale or a meter and pointer, the transmitting unit and a transducer fitted in the bottom of the yacht. (Fig. 4.7).

The principle of all echo sounders requires the instrument to measure the time taken for a short sound pulse to travel from the

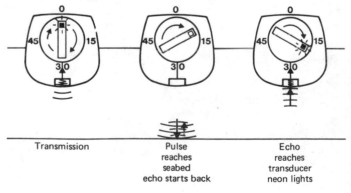

| Transmission | Pulse reaches seabed echo starts back | Echo reaches transducer neon lights |

HOW THE ECHO SOUNDER WORKS

Fig. 4.7

boat's transducer to the sea-bed and back. The time interval and hence the depth can be measured by using an arm which rotates at constant speed within the scale and holds a neon bulb at one end. As the bulb passes zero on the scale it flashes and also triggers the transmitting unit which applies a high frequency electrical pulse to the transducer, where it is converted into an ultrasonic sound pulse. This sound pulse is injected downwards into the sea where it travels at a constant velocity of 1500 metres per second (4920 feet per sec), strikes the sea bed and is returned as a weak echo at the same velocity to be "received" by the transducer. This converts the weak echo sound pulse back to an electrical pulse which is amplified and applied to the neon bulb on the rotating arm. This has moved round to a point proportional to the time taken for the pulse to travel down and back. The pulse causes the bulb to flash at this point which indicates the depth against the scale. The scale is calibrated to show depth, which is half the total distance travelled by the pulse in the time interval as shown by the expression:

$$\text{Depth (m)} = \frac{vt}{2}$$

where v is velocity of sound in salt water (m/sec)
t is time interval for pulse out and echo back. (secs)

As the pulses are made at a rapid rate, e.g. 400 per minute for deep soundings, and 2400 per minute for shallow, on one instrument, the neon flashes appear as a continuous bright line at zero and at the measured depth.

In instruments using meter and pointer presentation, the time difference between transmission of a pulse and reception of its echo is measured by electronic circuits which deliver a current to the meter proportional to the time difference and hence to the water depth.

Another type of echo sounder records the depth on sensitised paper by applying the electrical pulse created by the returning echo to a stylus which moves across the paper at a constant rate. The pulse burns away the surface of the paper at the appropriate place to leave a black line which is compared with a depth scale to obtain the sounding. The paper is made to move slowly so that a continuous record is obtained. (Fig. 4.8).

Sailing yachts should be fitted ideally with two transducers, one on each side of the keel, and with an automatic gravity operated switch to connect the lee side (deeper) transducer to the indicator. Aeration of the water immediately beneath the transducer may prevent sounding completely, and to avoid this, special transducers which project 50mm (2in) or more below the outer surface of the

Fig. 4.8   Neon Recording Echo Sounder (Courtesy of Electronic Laboratories (Marine) Ltd., Poole)

hull can be obtained, together with a fairing block. Transducers should generally be sited about one third of length from forward, but in some power boats better results may be obtained when sited one quarter of length from aft. All should be clear of any hull projections which may cause turbulence and aeration of the water, e.g. discharges.

The usual presentation shows soundings up to 108 metres (60 fathoms), with an accuracy of about 5% of depth. The minimum sounding which can be obtained is usually about 0.7 metre (2.5 feet). A control is often provided for adjustment to allow for the fact that the transducer is below sea level and enable the true depth of water to be displayed.

When the sounder is operating in deeper water than the maximum of the scale provided, e.g. sounding in 120 metres with maximum scale for one revolution of 100 metres, and if the sea bed is hard, it is possible for an echo to be returned to the transducer after the next pulse has been transmitted. In these circumstances a sounding may be indicated at 20 metres with the rotating arm making its next revolution. The time measured will be proportional to one and one fifth revolutions, so that the real depth indicated is 120 metres. Such echoes are called "second trace" echoes and they can be removed by decreasing gain. If they occur when using the sounder on shallow setting, e.g. sounding in 24 metres, maximum of scale 20 metres, sounder showing 4 metres, changing the phase switch to deep will usually confirm the proper depth which would then show as 24 metres on a 0 to 100 metre scale.

Fish, layers of water of differing salinity, and layers of plankton may also return echoes above the bottom echoes. In some circumstances they can completely mask the bottom echo.

RADIO RECEIVERS AND DIRECTION-FINDERS. A radio receiver is of great value aboard a yacht as it can be used to obtain weather forecasts. An ordinary portable set is not usually suitable for use at sea because it is liable to be damaged by sea air and damp, nevertheless it would be better to carry one of this type (provided it can receive on the Long Wave Band) rather than none at all. If it can be enclosed in a plastic covering and connected to a vertical aerial, it will probably give reasonable reception.

A number of small portable sets are made which combine the functions of radio receivers and direction-finders. These receivers operate off dry batteries or torch cells and they are designed for use in small craft. When connected to a vertical aerial (an insulated

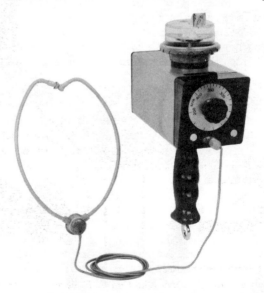

Fig. 4.9   C. Seafix (Electronic Laboratories (Marine) Ltd., Poole)

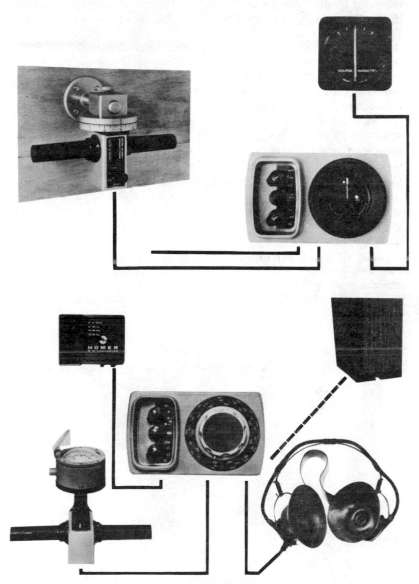

Fig. 4.9   A. Helios Radio Compass with Heron "E" (Brooks & Gatehouse Ltd.)   B. Homer Receiver, Heron D.F. Aerial and Homer Short-Wave Convertor (Brookes & Gatehouse Ltd.)

copper wire run up the mast is suitable) they can receive the general weather forecast for shipping broadcast by the B.B.C. on the Long Wave Band, and also local area forecasts on the Trawler Band.

As regards direction finding, these receivers may be divided into two types. One type is usually fixed in a suitable position in the yacht, and has either a vertical loop aerial or a horizontal ferrite rod mounted so that it is free to rotate about a vertical axis through the centre of the bearing plate secured to the top of the set. Relative bearings are obtained and are applied to the yacht's course. The other type is virtually a hand held radio bearing compass. It incorporates a horizontal ferrite rod and a bearing compass, so that compass bearings are directly obtained. (Fig. 4.9). The procedure for taking bearings with this equipment is described on page 108.

Chapter 5

Compass Errors and Corrections

Errors of the Compass

It is first necessary to understand the meaning of the following terms:
THE BOAT'S HEAD OR HEADING describes the direction in which the boat is pointing at any particular time.
THE COURSE describes the direction in which the boat is being, or is to be steered.
A BEARING is the direction of one position from another position.

Each of these directions can be described by referring it to the direction of one of the following datum lines through the boat's position:

1. The True Meridian, whose direction is described as True North.
2. The Magnetic Meridian, whose direction is described as Magnetic North.
3. The Axis of the Compass needles, whose direction is described as Compass North.

Hence directions referred to in:

1. are true courses and bearings, and are indicated by the suffix T.
2. are magnetic courses and bearings, and are indicated by the suffix M.
3. are compass courses and bearings, and are indicated by the suffix C.

These are usually given in degrees in the "3 figure notation".

060°T means a direction 60 degrees to the right of true north.

075°M means a direction 75 degrees to the right of magnetic north.

135°C means a direction 135 degrees to the right of compass north.

To an observer in a boat when out of sight of land, the horizon appears as a circle with the boat at its centre, and there is nothing to distinguish one point on that circle from another. In order to head the boat in a particular direction, and then to keep her heading in that direction, it is necessary to refer to some datum line or reference point.

This is supplied by the N. – S. line on the compass card, the N. point indicating the direction of compass north. Compass north does not generally lie in the same direction as true north because of the errors of variation and deviation which will now be described.

VARIATION. If a compass is placed in a boat constructed entirely of non-magnetic materials so that the compass needles are influenced by the earth's magnetic field and no other, the card will steady with its N. – S. line in the direction of the magnetic meridian through the boat's position, with the N. point of the card towards magnetic north. The magnetic and true meridians at a place do not generally coincide, because the earth's magnetic field is irregular, and the earth's N. and S. magnetic poles do not coincide with the geographical poles. The magnetic poles are areas about 50 miles in diameter which are constantly moving in unknown paths because the earth's magnetic field is continuously changing. In 1965 the magnetic poles were situated in lat. $75\frac{1}{2}$°N., long. 100°W., and lat. $67\frac{1}{2}$°S., 140°E long.

The angle, expressed in degrees and minutes of arc, between the true and magnetic meridians at a place is called the Variation. It is named Easterly when the direction of magnetic north lies to the east or right of the true meridian, and Westerly when to the west or left of the true meridian.

Because of the movement of the magnetic poles, the variation at any place is not constant, but changes slowly year by year. In practice the navigator obtains the variation for a specified year, and its rate of change, either from the coastal chart which he is using or from a special chart which has lines, known as "isogonic lines", drawn through all positions which have equal variation.

On coastal charts this information is given across the E. – W. axes of the "compass roses" placed at various positions on the charts. A part of one of the special charts covering the United Kingdom and Europe is given in Reed's Nautical Almanac, and shown in Fig. 5.1. It can be seen from this chart that the isogonic lines are the thin lines trending roughly north-south in this region, and that the variation is west almost throughout the whole of the area shown. On the eastern edge is the agonic line, or line through places where variation is zero, and to the east of that, in the eastern Baltic, the

MAGNETIC VARIATION CHART, 1970

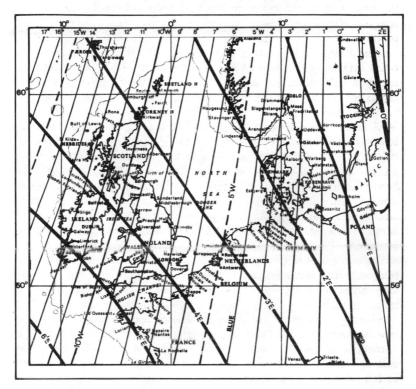

Reproduced from British Admiralty Chart No. 5375 with the permission of the Controller of H.M. Stationery Office and of the Hydrographer of the Navy

Fig. 5.1

variation is east. The wider lines trending roughly north west are called isallogonic lines and they are drawn through all places where the annual change of variation is constant. It can be seen from these lines that the westerly variation in the United Kingdom is decreasing by between 3' and 5' annually. Variation is found by first plotting the boat's position on this chart, and then taking the value from the nearest isogonic line. If the position comes between two lines, the value can be estimated by eye to the nearest half degree. This value is then corrected by adding or subtracting the change of variation, found by multiplying the rate of change in minutes of arc, by the difference in years between the specified and current year.

DEVIATION. If a magnetic compass is placed in a boat constructed of steel, or near to iron and steel fittings, or the engine, in a boat constructed of non-magnetic materials, the compass needles will almost certainly be deflected from the magnetic meridian through the boat's position, and the card will steady with its N. point towards the direction known as Compass North. The angle between the directions of magnetic north and compass north is called the Deviation. If compass north lies to the east or right of magnetic north, deviation is named Easterly: if it lies to the west or left, deviation is named Westerly. Deviation can also be caused in any boat if equipment such as loudspeakers, earphones, ammeters etc., which contain magnets, are placed too close to the compass.

Any iron or steel in a boat is partly magnetised by the earth's magnetic field during construction, and is further magnetised when she is in commission. The boat itself therefore acquires a magnetic field which unfortunately partly changes its direction and strength as the boat is turned onto different headings.

Deviation is caused by the boat's magnetic field acting at an angle to the compass needles, and because this angle and the strength of the boat's field change as the boat turns on to different headings, the deviation also changes with change of heading. It is therefore necessary to find the deviation when the boat is on each of a number of different headings, so that the correct deviation can be allowed when setting a course from one position to another.

One method of carrying out "a swing for deviation" is described below. This method which requires the use of a separate hand bearing compass, could be used in boats where it is impossible to take bearings from the steering compass because it is below the cockpit coaming.

SWINGING FOR DEVIATION. Before carrying out the swing, all movable iron, steel and electrical equipment should be stowed in its sea-going position, and as far away from the compass as possible.

The steering compass should be fixed, if possible, with its centre not less than the following distances from magnetic material:

Fixed magnetic material and other compasses	4 ft
Magnetic material occasionally moved	6 ft
Switches, headphones, loudspeakers, ammeters and other instruments containing small magnets	3 ft
Electric wiring should be twin-flex type if passing near to the compass.	

The compass should be fixed so that the two marks on the binnacle are in, or parallel to, the boat's fore and aft line, with the lubber line on the fore side of the compass bowl.

A calm day should be chosen, and the boat should be upright. The boat can be swung at anchor or on suitable moorings using extra lines run to a kedge anchor laid out astern, or better still, a kedge anchor laid out on each quarter. The swing should be carried out at or near slack water if any tidal stream is experienced at the anchorage or mooring. A line should be stretched from the top of the mast (if only one) to the centre of the transom, or alternatively two vertical battens should be temporarily set up over the boat's fore and aft line, one forward, and one aft. An assistant, with the hand bearing compass, should then be sent away in the dinghy after checking that it contains no iron or steel fittings. The dinghy should be positioned about three boat-lengths astern, and should adjust its position so that it remains astern of the boat throughout the swing. The boat is then slowly swung, adjusting the lines as necessary, and successively steadied on at least eight, but preferably sixteen, equidistant compass headings, e.g. say 000° (N.), 045° (N.E.), 090° (E.), and so on. As the boat is steadied and held on each heading, a previously agreed signal should be made to the dinghy, and the assistant there should immediately take a bearing of the boat's mast

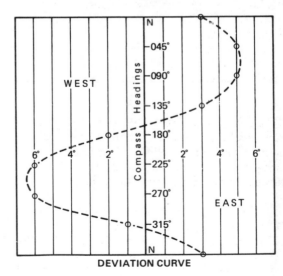

DEVIATION CURVE

Fig. 5.2

with the hand bearing compass when he sees the line stretched from the mast in line with the centre of the mast. (If battens have been erected this bearing should be taken when he sees them in line). The assistant then notes the bearing on a pad, signals that he has taken the bearing, and the boat is swung onto the next heading where the same routine is followed.

After the boat has been swung through 360°, which may have to be done in two parts if a strong tidal stream runs at the anchorage, the bearings taken from the dinghy should be compared with the corresponding compass headings of the boat noted during the swing. Each bearing taken from the dinghy can be assumed to be the magnetic heading of the boat at the time it was taken. The differences between corresponding compass and magnetic headings are the deviation on those headings, and they can be drawn up in a table (Table 5.1)

Table 5.1

Compass heading of boat		Deviation	Magnetic heading of boat
N.	000°C	3° E	003° M
N.E.	045°C	5° E	050° M
E.	090°C	5° E	095° M
S.E.	135°C	3° E	138° M
S.	180°C	2° W	178° M
S.W.	225°C	6° W	219° M
W.	270°C	6° W	264° M
N.W.	315°C	1° W	314° M

To name the deviations shown above, consider which way the steering compass card would have to be turned to achieve its corresponding magnetic heading. This will decide whether compass north lies to the left or right of magnetic north, and hence the name of the deviation.

Example. When the boat was heading 045°C., its magnetic heading was 050°M. To achieve a heading of 050° with the steering compass, the card would have to be turned to the left (anti-clockwise). Compass north must therefore lie to the right or east of magnetic north, and the deviation must be east on this heading. Similarly when the boat was heading 270°C, its magnetic heading was 264°M, and the compass card would have to be turned to the right (clockwise) to achieve 264°. Compass north must therefore lie to the left or west of magnetic north, and the deviation must be west on this heading.

These deviations can be plotted on graph paper to obtain a deviation curve as shown. (Fig. 5.2). The curve can then be used to obtain the deviations on other intermediate compass headings, say every 10° or 20°, and these together with the corresponding magnetic headings can be drawn up in a table for use in the boat. (Table 5.2).

Table 5.2

Compass	Deviation	Magnetic
000°C	3° E	003° M
020°C	4° E	024° M
040°C	5° E	045° M
060°C	5° E	065° M
080°C	5° E	085° M
100°C	5° E	105° M
120°C	4° E	124° M
140°C	3° E	143° M
160°C	Nil	160° M
180°C	2° W	178° M

Similar results can be obtained, perhaps more readily for a check swing, by using black plastic tape to make sighting marks on each side of the centre of the pulpit, in such a way that when viewed from right aft, the mast just fits between the marks when the observer is sighting directly along the fore and aft line. (If there is no pulpit lash a sighting bar with two similar marks to the forestay). If the boat is then put on successive headings, even moving about if necessary, and a bearing of the mast when it is centred between the marks is taken on each heading with the hand bearing compass held in as high a position as possible, a similar table to Table 5.2 can be prepared. The hand bearing compass observations would be assumed to be magnetic headings, and the equivalent compass headings of the boat would need to be noted as before.

If the boat is fitted with an engine, it would be as well to carry out a second swing with the engine running to see if the deviations are different on any headings, and if they are, a second card should be drawn up for use when the engine is running.

In sailing craft which may be heeled appreciably for long intervals when close hauled or reaching, the deviations on certain courses may differ from those obtained when upright. The amount of change of deviation on any heading through heeling, is known as heeling error, and if present is maximum on N. – S. courses, and nil on E. – W. courses. It may be possible to detect heeling error by heeling the boat with weights hung from the boom squared off at right angles to the fore and aft line, heading her N. or S. by compass, and then finding the deviation when heeled with the hand bearing compass as before. Any difference between the deviations on equivalent headings when heeled and upright is the heeling error. It is impossible to allow for heeling error, but a compass adjuster can counteract the force that causes it with suitably placed vertical magnets. Similarly, a compass adjuster can reduce deviations found when upright by placing small correctors near to the compass. It will probably be essential to have the deviations reduced in this way in a steel yacht.

A boat should be swung at least once per season, preferably at the beginning of the season if she has been laid up during the winter. During the season the deviations should be checked when possible by comparing the compass heading when the boat is sailing down a suitable transit, with the corresponding magnetic heading obtained from the chart.

CORRECTION OF COURSES AND BEARINGS. In practice the navigator has to work out the compass course to steer after he has obtained the required true or magnetic course from the chart. Alternatively, after steering a certain compass course for some time, he has to work out the corresponding magnetic or true course steered, so that he can estimate his position after allowing for the effects of wind and tidal stream. Similarly, compass bearings taken to fix the boat's position have to be converted into true or magnetic bearings before they can be drawn on the chart. To correct these various courses and bearings, the appropriate variation and deviation (if any) must be applied correctly and, to simplify this application, all courses and bearings should be expressed in the "3 figure notation".

TO FIND THE COMPASS COURSE TO STEER. A pencil line is first drawn or laid off in the required direction from the boat's position on the chart using the parallel rulers. These are then slid or rolled to the centre of the nearest compass rose. (A typical compass rose is shown in Fig. 5.3). The true course is then read from

Compass Roses, True and Magnetic

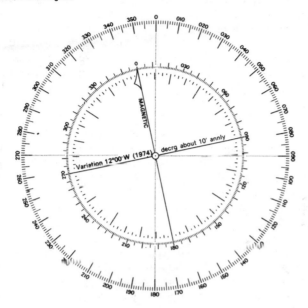

Reproduced from British Admiralty Chart No. 5011 with the permission of the Controller of H.M. Stationery Office and of the Hydrographer of the Navy

The figures in brackets after the variation denote the year for which it is given.

Fig. 5.3

where the rulers cut the outer circle of graduations, or the magnetic course from where the rulers cut the inner circle of graduations. It is advisable to use the outer true rose as it is clearer and easier to read, unless the boat's steering compass is marked only in points, and half or quarter points. If this is the case the magnetic course can be read from the inner markings of the inner magnetic rose. If the navigator prefers to start with the magnetic course from the chart this probably can be most easily achieved by drawing in waterproof coloured ink a series of magnetic meridians across the chart, each inclined to the true meridians at the appropriate variation for that area. He can then use the graduations on his parallel rules, Douglas protractor or other device to read, or lay off, magnetic courses and bearings directly against these magnetic meridians.

73

If the true course has been measured, it must be first converted to a magnetic course by applying the variation for the boat's position, after correcting it for any accumulated change of variation.

Example. In 1970 the variation off Penzance was 9° 15' W. decreasing about 5' annually. What is the variation to use in this area in 1973? (Check above variation on Variation chart shown on page 67).

The variation must be corrected for annual change, which here is 3 years at 5' per year equal to −15'.

1970 variation	9° 15' W.
3 years' change	−15'
1973 variation	9° 00' W. (*High*)

The variation should be normally corrected to the nearest whole degree, and then named *High* if west, and *Low* if east. The correction can be usually made mentally. (Note: The reason for naming the above westerly variation *High* can be seen by looking at the compass rose (Fig. 5.3) where it can be seen that all the magnetic values are higher than their equivalent true values by the amount of the variation which is there shown as 12° W.).

It must be clearly understood that the value of the variation depends on the boat's geographical position and this is clearly shown on the variation chart on page 67, where it can be seen that the variation off Stockholm for example is 1° E. and changing a negligible amount each year.

Deviation must also be considered, to simplify its application, all easterly deviations in the table should be marked *Low* (East − least − *Low*) and all westerly deviations marked *High*. It can be seen in the deviation table (Table 5.1) that when the deviations are expressed in this way, they indicate the number of degrees that the compass headings are either *Low* or *High* when compared with their corresponding magnetic headings. Therefore a *Low* variation should be subtracted from a true course to get a magnetic course, and a *Low* deviation subtracted from a magnetic course to get a compass course to steer. High variation and high deviation should be added to their respective headings to obtain magnetic and compass courses respectively.

The deviation is obtained from the table to the nearest degree by entering the column headed Magnetic with the magnetic course and estimating between successive values as necessary.

Example. Off Penzance, and using the variation of 9° W. (*High*) previously obtained, what compass course should be steered if the course obtained from the chart is 146° T., and the deviation table is that shown on page 71?

True course from chart	146° T.
Variation corrected for annual change	+9° W. (*High*)
Magnetic course to steer	155° M. (Higher than T.)
Deviation from table (see note 1 below)	−1° E. (*Low*)
Compass course to steer	154° C. (Lower than M.)

Note 1: Deviation is 3° E. (*Low*) on 143° M. and *Nil* on 160° M. and it therefore changes 1° for approximately 6° change of heading. Because 155° M. is 5° from 160° M. the deviation on 155° M. differs by 1° from that on 160° M. giving 1° E. (*Low*).

Note 2: The order of application of variation and deviation when converting true to compass is:

true variation magnetic deviation compass.

Note 3: Where variation is *High* the magnetic course is higher than true. Where deviation is *Low* the compass course is lower than magnetic and vice-versa. In other words, when error is high steer high, when low steer low.

Note 4: The sum of variation and deviation is here 9° W. (*High*) plus 1° E. (*Low*) equal to 8° W. (*High*), and is called the compass error. The compass course is therefore 8° higher than the true course.

TO FIND THE TRUE OR MAGNETIC COURSE STEERED AFTER STEERING A CERTAIN COMPASS COURSE. When a yacht is sailing as close to the wind as possible, first on one tack and then on the other, the average compass course steered on each tack must be noted by the helmsman, so that it can be converted into its corresponding true or magnetic course and laid off on the chart from the yacht's last known or estimated position. The appropriate deviation is obtained from the table to the nearest degree, by entering the column headed Compass with the compass course steered, and interpolating between successive values as necessary. If the deviation obtained is low, this indicates that the compass reading was low, and the deviation must be added to obtain the magnetic course steered; if high, this indicates that the compass reading was high, and it must be subtracted.

For those plotting using magnetic information, the magnetic course can be now laid off from the boat's last known position using the magnetic rose or magnetic meridian drawn on the chart.

COMPASS ERRORS AND CORRECTIONS

In all other cases the corrected variation must be applied to the magnetic course in order to obtain the true course which has been steered. The parallel rules can then be laid across the nearest true rose at the appropriate true course and then moved to the boat's last position to draw in the true course steered.

Example. Off Dublin in 1975, steering 105°C., deviation as per table on page 71, variation 10° 20′ W. (1970) decreasing about 4′. annually. What is the true course to lay off on the chart from the yacht's position?

By inspection of the deviation card, it can be seen that the deviation on 105°C. is 4¾°E. (*Low*), or 5°E. (*Low*) to the nearest degree. The variation is 10° 20′ W. less 5 × 4′ per year equal to 20′, to give 10°W. (*High*). The calculation is then:

Compass course steered	105°C.	
Deviation (from table)	+5°E. (*Low*)	(Added because C. is low compared to M.)
Magnetic course steered	110°M.	
Variation	−10°W. (*High*)	(Subtracted because M. is higher than T.)
True course steered	100°T.	

Note 1: Order of application of errors is:
   compass   deviation   magnetic   variation   true.
Note 2: The compass error is 5°E. (*Low*) plus 10°W. (*High*) equal to 5°W. (*High*). The compass course is therefore 5° higher than the true course, and the error must be subtracted to give the true course.

BEARINGS. A hand bearing compass is usually used for taking bearings from small yachts as the steering compass is normally sited low down in the boat and from its position it is not possible to take bearings. If the bearings are taken with the hand compass from a carefully chosen position in the cockpit, as far away as possible from rigging and other steel fittings, meters etc., they may be regarded as magnetic bearings, and after variation has been applied to them as shown above, the true bearings obtained can be drawn on the chart using the true rose. Suitable observing positions can be found for this compass by taking bearings of two visible charted objects when they are in line from several different positions in the cockpit. Those suitable are the positions from which the observed bearings agree with their correct magnetic bearings taken from the chart.

In some large yachts, the compass used for taking bearings is fixed to the cabin top or doghouse roof, and may in this position be subject to deviation. A deviation table must be provided for such a compass, and any bearings taken from it must be corrected in the manner described previously, before being laid off on the chart. It is essential to bear in mind that the deviation used for correcting a compass bearing must be that appropriate to the Boat's Head at the time the bearing was taken.

For example: Assuming that the compass bearing of a light was 180° C., with the boat heading 040° C., then if the deviation table on page 71 was correct for this particular compass, the deviation to apply to the bearing would be 5° *Low* (that given for 040° C.) and *not* 2° *High* (that given for 180° C.). The magnetic bearing would therefore be 185° M.

Chapter 6

Laying a Course

The Track describes the path along which the boat has moved, or the path along which it is desired she should move. It often differs from the course because of the effects of wind and tidal streams.

LEEWAY. Except when she is sailing with the wind abaft the beam, a sailing yacht, besides moving forwards, will be pushed sideways by the pressure of the wind on her sails, hull and gear. A power driven yacht will be similarly affected except when the wind is from ahead or from astern. This sideways movement, known as leeway, is expressed as an angle in degrees, and is the angle between the course that the yacht is steering, and the track that she is making good through the water. The amount of leeway made will depend on the yacht's draught, freeboard and speed, the strength and direction of the wind relative to her course, and the state of the sea. Yachts with shallow draught or high freeboard will make more than those with deep draught or low freeboard, and a yacht close hauled will probably make more than one reaching. The amount can only be estimated, and this may be done by obtaining a magnetic bearing of the farthest visible part of the wake, or of the direction of the logline, reversing the bearing by adding or subtracting 180°, and

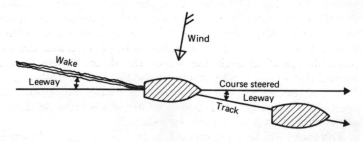

Fig. 6.1

comparing the result with the boat's magnetic course. In power driven yachts and sailing yachts when reaching, any leeway made, once it has been estimated, can be counteracted by steering a course to windward of that obtained from the chart. (Fig. 6.1).

Example: Course obtained from the chart 085° T., wind North (note: Wind is named by direction *From* which it blows), estimated leeway 5°. The course to steer to make good 085° T. is therefore 080° T. (085° −5°). Leeway cannot be allowed for in this way when a yacht is sailing close-hauled, and her course made good will therefore be to leeward of that steered. The amount made must be noted and then applied to leeward of the course steered when plotting the yacht's track on the chart.

Example: A yacht has steered a course of 100° T,. when close hauled, wind N.E., estimated leeway 3°. Her track through the water is therefore 103° T. (100° + 3°).

THE EFFECTS OF TIDAL STREAMS. When a tidal stream is running directly with, or against a yacht, her speed made good over the ground is equal to the sum of, or difference between, her speed through the water and the rate of the stream. If the stream is against a yacht, and its rate is more than her speed through the water, she will be carried backwards in the opposite direction to the course that she is steering. No allowance need be made when setting the course, but when from time to time the yacht's position has to be plotted on the chart, the distance that the stream has carried her forward or set her back, will have to be added to, or subtracted from, the distance sailed as shown by the log.

A stream setting obliquely across the yacht's course will carry her bodily in the direction that the stream is setting, and her track made good will be to one side or the other of her course steered by an amount that depends on her speed through the water and the rate and direction of the stream. Because of the generally low speeds of yachts, this effect must always be considered before setting a course. Bearing in mind the distance to be covered and the yacht's probable speed through the water the direct course should be steered if it appears, after studying the tidal stream atlas, that the effects of the stream will cancel out, or nearly cancel out, in the course of the passage, and there is plenty of sea room on either side of the direct line between the two places.

The yacht will be set to one side of the direct line, and then back, but the distance she will sail will be shorter than if she had counteracted the stream throughout the passage. Naturally it is rare that the effects of the stream exactly cancel out, but the practice should be, let as much as possible cancel out and then counteract for the rest of the passage. If, on the other hand, it appears that the stream will set generally in one direction throughout the passage, or if the proposed track takes the yacht close to some danger, then the tidal stream effect must be allowed for when setting the course.

To Find the Course to Steer Allowing for the Tidal Stream
Assuming, for example, that a passage has to be made from the South Goodwin Lightvessel to a buoy off Calais, and that it is estimated that under the conditions existing at the time, the yacht will sail at 5 knots through the water, what is the true course to steer for the first three hours allowing for the tidal stream?

The track to be made good is found by drawing a line on the chart between the lightvessel and the buoy, and the distance by measuring along this line with the dividers, using the latitude scale. In this example the track is found to be 130° T. and the distance 15 miles.

The tidal stream tables on the chart for the lettered positions B, E and N are then examined, and from these it is estimated that the stream will set 227° T. at 2.0 knots, 220° T. at 2.7 knots, and 239° T. at 1.5 knots, for the first, second and third hours respectively. The directions and the distances that the yacht would be carried by the stream if it experienced each prediction in turn for one hour, are then laid off from the starting point S, using any convenient scale (See Fig. 6.2). The line SABC then represents the estimated total drift of the stream in three hours.

Then, having set the dividers or compasses, using the same scale, to the distance that the yacht is expected to sail in 3 hours (i.e. 15 units), place one leg at the end of the drift at C, and make a mark at F where the other leg cuts the track to be made good. Then C to F represents the direction to steer from S and, if the parallel rulers are laid in this direction, and then moved to the nearest rose, the true course (106° T.) can be found, and by applying variation and deviation, the compass course. The distance SF, to the same scale, represents the distance (13 miles) the yacht should make good in 3 hours.

Alternatively, when the stream is setting roughly in the same direction throughout, the directions and rates can be averaged, in this example 229° T. at 2 knots, and a triangle of velocities (MNP) drawn based on a time interval of 1 hour. MN then represents the average direction and rate of the stream, NP the direction to steer

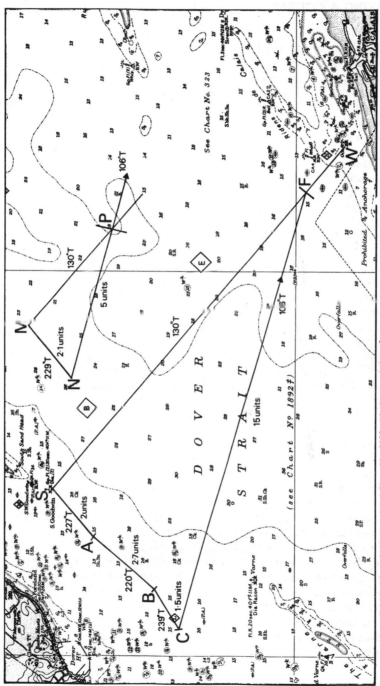

Reproduced from British Admiralty Instructional Chart No. 5066 with the permission of the Controller of H.M. Stationery Office and of the Hydrographer of the Navy.

Fig. 6.2

(106° T.) and MP the average speed the yacht should make good (4.3 knots).

The above construction, for finding the course to steer, can be done on any convenient part of the chart, as long as the lines which represent the track and the drift of the stream are drawn in their correct directions.

If, after the yacht has been set on her course, it is estimated that she is making leeway, then the course should be adjusted as described previously, so that she steers to windward of the course set to counteract the stream. The correctness of the course steered in this example could be checked at first by taking back bearings of the lightvessel while it remained visible, and laying them off on the chart. If the course is correct, or nearly so, the bearings will very nearly coincide with the proposed track. It must be clearly understood that for the yacht to make good the required track, she must sail at the estimated speed used in the plot (in this case 5 knots), and the tidal stream must set exactly as predicted. In practice this is unlikely to occur, but the yacht should nearly make good her track as long as her speed is near that estimated. It may be, however, because of variations in the wind's strength and direction, or perhaps some mechanical fault in power driven craft, that after 2 hours on the course set in this example the yacht has logged only 8 miles instead of 10 miles. It will then be necessary to estimate the yacht's position, and find the new course to steer from this position to the destination.

Chapter 7

Position Fixing

To Plot a Yacht's Estimated Position

Assuming that after 2 hours the yacht in the previous example has
logged 8 miles after steering 111° T. (117° M.) to counteract leeway
estimated at 5°, wind south, what is her dead reckoning and estimated
position, if the tidal stream predictions for the first two hours
are as before?

First apply the leeway downwind of the course steered, to find
the course made good through the water. (This step is missed out if
there is no leeway).

Course steered	111° T.	(117° M.)
Leeway	−5°	−5°
Course made good through water	106° T.	(112° M.)

Lay off this course from S, using the true (or magnetic) rose, and
then having set the dividers to a distance of 8 miles on the latitude
scale, place one leg at S and make a mark at G where the other leg
cuts the course (see Fig. 7.1). The point G is called a Dead Reckoning
position (D.R.), and should be marked with a cross +, the log
reading and the time. Such a position takes account only of the
course made good through the water and the boat's speed through
the water.

Now from G lay off the predicted directions and drifts of the
stream for the first and second hours, i.e. 227° for 2 miles (GH),
and 220° T. for 2.7 miles (HK). The point K is the yacht's Estimated
Position (E.P.) 2 hours after leaving the lightvessel. This point should
have a small triangle marked to enclose it to indicate that it is an
estimated position, and the log reading and the time should be
marked against it. SK is the estimated track and distance made
good, and KW the new track and distance to make good from K.

A yacht's estimated position should be plotted in this way at
regular intervals, whenever she is making a passage out of sight of

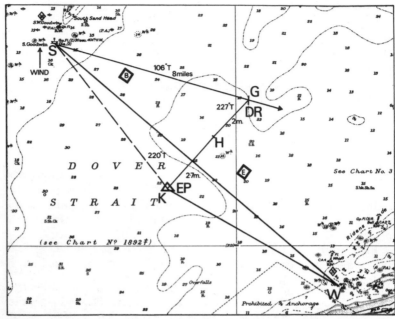

Reproduced from British Admiralty Instructional Chart No. 5066 with the permission of the
Controller of H.M. Stationery Office and of the Hydrographer of the Navy

Fig. 7.1

land, and her position cannot be fixed by bearings or other methods
(see later notes).

To Fix a Yacht's Position by Observation

While a yacht is making a passage along a coast, her position
should be ascertained at regular intervals in order that her navigator
may be sure that she is following her planned track. This is done
when the yacht is close enough to the land by observing landmarks,
and from these observations obtaining what are known as "position
lines". A position line is any straight or curved line drawn on the
chart on which the yacht's position is known to lie. The easiest way
of obtaining a position line is by using the hand bearing compass to
observe the bearing of a lighthouse (or a beacon, a lightvessel or
other charted landmark) and then, on the chart, drawing a pencil
line towards the charted position of the lighthouse in the same direction as the bearing.

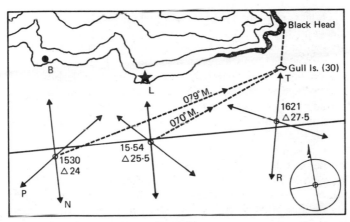

Fig. 7.2

Suppose, for example, that at 1530, the lighthouse L in Fig. 7.2 bears 060° M. and variation 10° W. (*High*). The true bearing is then 050° T. If the parallel rules are laid across the nearest compass rose in the direction 050° T. (060° M.), and are then slid across the chart until one edge lies through L, then the line PL drawn in the direction of 050° T. (060° M.) towards L is a position line. The yacht must lie somewhere on this line, because it runs through all the possible positions from which the lighthouse could bear 050° T. If at the same time, the beacon B bears 003° M., which is 353° T., then a second position line BN can be drawn as before, and the yacht must also lie on this line for the same reason. The point of intersection of the two lines PL and BN, ringed with a small circle, is the only point from which these two bearings could have been observed, and therefore represents the yacht's position at 1530. Such a position is called a "fix", and it should have marked against it the time of observation and the log reading at that time, as shown in the figure. A log reading is shown on the chart by marking the reading against a small triangle (e.g. in this case the reading is assumed to be 24). Another fix is shown for 1554 when the lighthouse and beacon were assumed to be bearing 005° M. and 317° M. respectively (355° T. and 307° T. respectively).

When a yacht's position is fixed by two bearings, the objects chosen, should, if possible, be placed so that their bearings differ by nearly 90°, because the effect of any possible small errors in the taking, or laying off of the bearings is thus decreased. If two position lines cut at an angle of less than 30°, the fix should not be relied upon. Objects near the yacht should always be chosen in preference to objects far away.

The technique of taking bearings requires practice. The line across the compass, on the prism and the notch should all be in line as the bearing is taken. It will take time and probably require a mental average of readings at night, as a light may only show at 20 second intervals, and each time it appears the boat will have moved slightly, and the prism will no longer be lined up with the light. (See Fig. 4.3A).

When coasting a navigator should always be looking ahead for landmarks suitable for fixing his yacht. Quite often suitable landmarks, such as hills, islets, chimneys, churches, etc., are visible, but cannot be clearly identified on the chart. Such a landmark can usually be identified by fixing the yacht at least twice by means of known objects, and on each occasion simultaneously taking a bearing of the unknown object. If two or more such bearings are laid off from their respective fixes, the unidentified object will probably be found on the chart close to the point where the bearings intersect. *Example.* In the previous example, a small island was seen to be bearing 079° M. at 1530 and 070° M. at 1554. When laid off from their respective fixes, these two bearings (the dotted lines) cut close to Gull Island, and thus identified it.

On the same figure, the third fix at 1621 illustrates a transit, which is another method of obtaining a position line. If an observer sees two objects in line, then he must be situated somewhere on the line joining them, produced in his direction. An excellent position line is obtained in this way, when the observer's distance from the nearer object is not more than about three times the distance

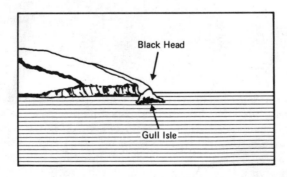

Fig. 7.3

between the objects. In this example, the centre of Gull Island was seen to be in line with Black Head at 1621, (as shown in Fig. 7.3) and the line TR represents the position line obtained. At the same time, the lighthouse L bore 297° M., and this fixed the yacht's position when laid off on the chart.

Transit lines are often drawn on charts to act as clearing lines as shown on the portion of chart in Fig. 7.4. They are ideal for use when the boat is being conned through a channel, particularly when the tidal stream is setting across the boat's course. They enable quick adjustments to be made to the boat's course to keep her on the safe track without the necessity of a large number of bearings.

When a fix is obtained from bearings of three objects, their bearings should, if possible, differ by about 60° to give the best angle of cut. The three objects should either lie on, or nearly on, the same straight line, or the centre object should be nearer the yacht than a line joining the other two, or the yacht should lie within the triangle formed by lines joining the three objects.

When three bearings are taken, the resulting position will not as a rule meet in a point; they will form a triangle, which is known as a "cocked hat". If the cocked hat is small, the yacht's position can usually be taken as its centre. If it is large, and a check has revealed no error in taking or laying off the bearings, the yacht's position should be taken as the corner of the cocked hat which will place her nearest to danger.

If there is any doubt about whether deviation is affecting the hand compass bearings, the boat's position can be fixed if three suitably placed charted objects (see above) can be seen, by observing the horizontal angles between pairs of objects in quick succession. The angles can be measured using the hand bearing compass in one chosen place in the cockpit with the boat on constant heading, or by using a sextant held horizontally, if one is carried in the boat. The method using the hand bearing compass is described here, as it can be used to check whether the hand bearing compass is being affected by deviation, and if so, by how much.

Example. Assuming a yacht is in Mounts Bay and takes the following bearings using the hand bearing compass which it is feared is being affected by the yacht's magnetic field which is causing deviation:

The yacht is steady on a course of 135° M.

A	Tater-du lighthouse	284° C.
B	St. Clements Island	322° C.
C	St. Michael's Mount Tower	016° C.

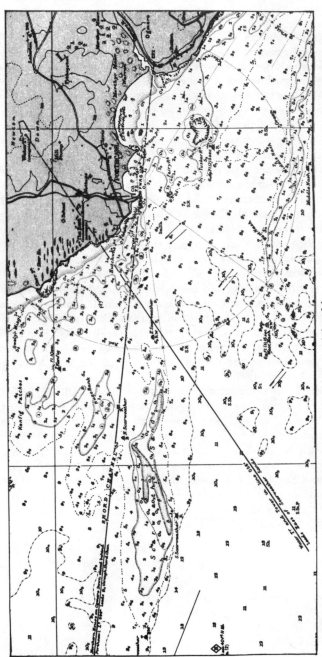

Reproduced from British Admiralty Instructional Chart No. 5062 with the permission of the Controller of H.M. Stationery Office and of the Hydrographer of the Navy

Fig. 7.4

It is required that the yacht's position is plotted using the method of horizontal angles, and that the hand bearing compass position is checked for deviation, assuming variation is 9° W.

The horizontal angles must be obtained first by subtracting the first bearing from the second, and the second from the third.

B	St. Clements Island		322° C.
A	Tater-du lighthouse		− 284° C.
	Left hand angle		38°
C	St. Michael's Mount Tr. 016° + 360°	=	376° C.
B	St. Clements Island		− 322° C.
	Right hand angle		54°

The terms left hand and right hand angles refer to the way the observer would see them.

There are four methods of plotting these angles to obtain the position. These are:

1. Use a station pointer by setting the left hand and right hand movable arms to the above angles respectively; place the station pointer on the chart and move about until the arms align themselves with the objects, and then mark the position at the centre of the station pointer. (Fig. 7.5).

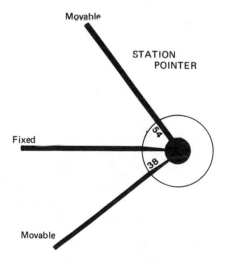

Fig. 7.5

2. Draw the bearing lines on tracing paper or a Douglas protractor at the observed angles, place on the chart and move about until the lines align themselves with the objects. Mark the chart at the intersection of the lines to give the position. (Note: The Douglas protractor has a matt surface to enable lines to be drawn on it.) (Fig. 7.6).

3. Use tables in Reed's Nautical Almanac to obtain radii of the two position circles, and plot the circles to obtain the position. (See Reeds for details.)

4. Plot geometrically using a protractor and compasses to draw the intersecting position line circles.

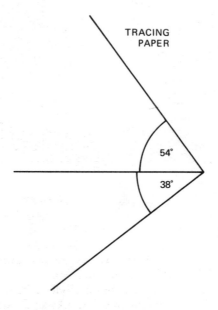

TRACING
PAPER

54°

38°

Fig. 7.6

The fourth method is described here in detail and shown in Fig. 7.7.

The position lines obtained from horizontal angles are two circles passing through the left hand and right hand pairs of objects and the yacht's position. In order to plot the position circles, the construction must define the centre of each circle. The method is as follows:

Reproduced from British Admiralty Chart No. 777 with the permission of the Controller of
H.M. Stationery Office and of the Hydrographer of the Navy

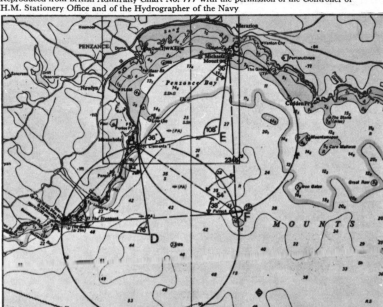

Fig. 7.7

1. Subtract each horizontal angle from 90° to obtain the "base" angles of the "centre" triangle. Here the "base" angles are:
   Left hand: 90° − 38° = 52°
   Right hand: 90° − 54° = 36°
2. Join the three objects by two straight lines, i.e. from A to B, and from B to C, by pencil lines.
3. To construct the left hand circle, take a protractor, and at A and B, draw two lines from A and B, inclined to AB at the left hand "base" angle, to intersect at D. D is the centre of the left hand circle, of radius AD, which can now be drawn through A and B. (see figure).
4. Construct the right hand circle by the same method, by taking the protractor, and at B and C, drawing two lines from B and C, inclined to BC at the right hand "base" angles, to intersect at E. E is the centre of the right hand circle of radius BE. This can now be drawn through B and C, to cut the left hand circle in F, which is the required position.

Note: The reasoning behind this construction involves the geometric theorems which say that:

a. The 3 angles of a triangle sum to 180°; e.g. triangle ABD, so that angle BDA equals 76°.

b. The angle at the centre of a circle is equal to twice the angle at the circumference standing on the same arc. (AB), e.g. angle BDA = 76° = 2 × angle BFA. Therefore angle BFA = 38° equals the observed left hand angle.

c. Angles, in the same segment of a circle are equal. Therefore angle BFA, equal to 38°, would be obtained from any position on the circle ABF, and therefore satisfies the requirements of a position line.

From position F the true bearing of Tater-du is found to be 265° T., and therefore the magnetic bearing is 265° T. + 9° W. (*High*) equal to 274° M. The compass bearing was 284° C. and therefore that compass position is subject to deviation of 284° C. − 274° M. = 10° W. (*High*) when on that particular course of 135° M.

If the yacht is inside the triangle formed by joining the three points, A, B and C in Fig. 7.8, the angles observed between A and B, and B and C will be greater than 90°, e.g. in Fig. 7.8 showing possible D.F. bearings of Cape Barfleur, Portland Bill and St. Catherine's Point the bearings were assumed to be:

A	Cape Barfleur	165° C.
B	Portland Bill	299° C.
C	St. Catherine's Point	049° C.

making the angles A to B 134°, and B to C 110°. To plot these angles as shown, follow the instructions as before, so that the "base" angles will be:

Left hand: 90° − 134° = − 44°.
Right hand: 90° − 110° = − 20°.

Take the above negative "base" angles as an indication that the yacht and the centre of each circle are on opposite sides of lines joining the places AB and BC. The only difference to the further instructions is to 3 and 4. These require, in 3 the "base" angle −44° to be drawn to the westward of AB, and the "base" angle − 20° to be drawn on the land side of BC, to produce the two centres of the circles.

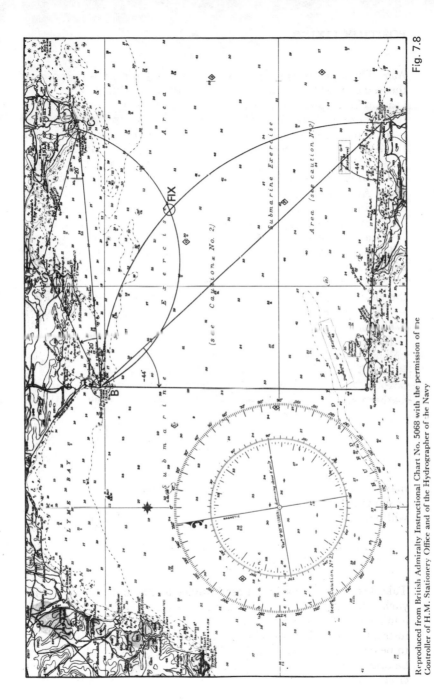

Fig. 7.8

Reproduced from British Admiralty Instructional Chart No. 5068 with the permission of the Controller of H.M. Stationery Office and of the Hydrographer of the Navy

RISING AND DIPPING DISTANCES. An approximate position line can be obtained at night when making a landfall, or when leaving the coast, by noting the time when a light with sufficient intensity first appears above the horizon, or dips below the horizon when going away from the light. The yacht's approximate distance from the light can then be calculated.

This distance is called the Geographical range, and is the maximum distance at which the light can theoretically reach an observer when limited only by the earth's curvature, normal atmospheric refraction, and by the elevation of the light and the observer's height of eye. The method should not be used therefore when there is abnormal refraction, which may be recognised by apparent mirage effects, or by raising the light at excessive range. The time at which the light appears or dips can be recognised if the observer changes the height at which he is keeping a lookout. The method is not an easy one to use in a yacht, because of its movement, and the range obtained should be regarded as approximate. The position line obtained in this way is a circle whose radius is equal to the yacht's distance from the light.

The range is obtained by adding the yacht's distance from the horizon, to the distance of the light beyond the horizon (see Fig. 7.9). These two distances can be found by entering a "Distance of Sea Horizon" table or "Geographical Range" table, with the observer's height of eye above the sea in metres or feet, and the elevation of the light, obtained from the chart, Light List or Almanac. (Tables 7.1/2). Such a table is contained in all Light Lists, and in Reed's Nautical Almanac. Because a light's charted height is given above MHWS, a distance obtained by using this height

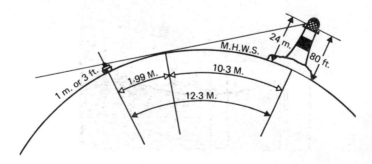

Fig. 7.9

may be too small if the height of the tide at the time is much below MHWS. If maximum accuracy is required the estimated amount that the tide is below MHWS should be added to the charted height of the light before entering the table. The power of a light must be considered before using this method, and it must not be used if the charted range is less than the range by calculation. When a light first appears above the horizon, the yacht's movement in the seaway will increase and decrease the observer's height of eye (unless the sea is smooth) and may make the light's characteristic appear different from that charted. Before plotting the position line therefore, sufficient time should be allowed for the yacht to move clearly within range of the light, so that its characteristic can be properly checked.

If a bearing is taken as soon as the light rises or dips, the yacht's position lies where the two position lines intersect (see Fig. 7.10).

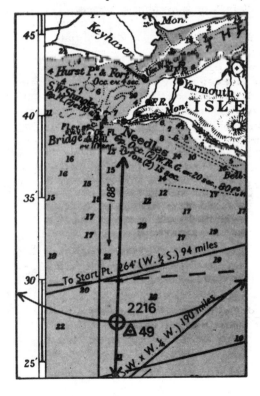

Fig. 7.10

Example. At 2216 log 49 when approaching Needles lighthouse from the south, its white light was raised bearing 002° T. (009° M.). The observer's height of eye was 1 metre (3 feet) above the sea and the light's elevation was charted as 24 metres (80 feet). Its charted range (nominal) was 17 miles. It is required to fix the yacht's position.

The Distance of the Sea Horizon table gives:

Distance of yacht from horizon (H.E. 3 ft.)	1.99 miles.
Distance of light beyond horizon (Ht. 80 ft.)	10.3 miles.
Distance of yacht from light (approx.)	12.29 miles.

As an alternative, entering the Geographical range table with 1 metre in the top line and 24 metres down the side, gives the range as 12.0 miles (approximately).

DISTANCE OF SEA HORIZON
IN NAUTICAL MILES

Height in Feet	Distance in Miles	Height in Feet	Distance in Miles	Height in Feet	Distance in Miles	Height in Feet	Distance in Miles	Height in Feet	Distance in Miles
1	1·15	14	4·30	27	5·97	40	7·27	65	9·3
2	1·62	15	4·45	28	6·08	41	7·36	70	9·6
3	1·99	16	4·60	29	6·18	42	7·44	75	10·0
4	2·30	17	4·73	30	6·30	43	7·54	80	10·3
5	2·57	18	4·87	31	6·40	44	7·62	85	10·6
6	2·81	19	5·01	32	6·50	45	7·70	90	10·9
7	3·04	20	5·14	33	6·60	46	7·79	95	11·2
8	3·25	21	5·26	34	6·70	47	7·88	100	11·5
9	3·45	22	5·39	35	6·80	48	7·96	120	12·6
10	3·63	23	5·51	36	6·90	49	8·0	130	13·1
11	3·81	24	5·62	37	6·99	50	8·1	140	13·6
12	3·98	25	5·74	38	7·09	55	8·5	150	14·1
13	4·14	26	5·86	39	7·17	60	8·9	160	14·5

Table 7.1

If the geographical range exceeds the charted (nominal) range, the light is not powerful enough for this method to be used. The yacht's approximate position in this example is therefore 182° T., 12.0 miles from the Needles lighthouse.

Table 7.2

GEOGRAPHICAL RANGE TABLE

Elevation in		Height of Eye of Observer in feet/**metres**							
ft		3	7	10	13	16	20	23	26
	m	**1**	**2**	**3**	**4**	**5**	**6**	**7**	**8**
				Range in Sea Miles					
0	0	2·0	2·9	3·5	4·1	4·5	5·0	5·4	5·7
3	1	4·1	4·9	5·5	6·1	6·6	7·0	7·4	7·8
7	2	4·9	5·7	6·4	6·9	7·4	7·8	8·2	8·6
10	3	5·5	6·4	7·0	7·6	8·1	8·5	8·9	9·3
13	4	6·1	6·9	7·6	8·1	8·6	9·0	9·4	9·8
10	5	6·6	7·4	8·1	8·6	9·1	9·5	9·9	10·3
20	6	7·0	7·8	8·5	9·0	9·5	9·9	10·3	10·7
23	7	7·4	8·2	8·9	9·4	9·9	10·3	10·7	11·1
26	8	7·8	8·6	9·3	9·8	10·3	10·7	11·1	11·5
30	9	8·1	9·0	9·6	10·2	10·6	11·1	11·5	11·8
33	10	8·5	9·3	9·9	10·5	11·0	11·4	11·8	12·2
36	11	8·8	9·6	10·3	10·8	11·3	11·7	12·1	12·5
39	12	9·1	9·9	10·6	11·1	11·6	12·0	12·4	12·8
43	13	9·4	10·2	10·8	11·4	11·9	12·3	12·7	13·1
46	14	9·6	10·5	11·1	11·7	12·1	12·6	13·0	13·3
49	15	9·9	10·7	11·4	11·9	12·4	12·8	13·2	13·6
52	16	10·2	11·0	11·6	12·2	12·7	13·1	13·5	13·9
56	17	10·4	11·2	11·9	12·4	12·9	13·3	13·7	14·1
59	18	10·6	11·5	12·1	12·7	13·2	13·6	14·0	14·4
62	19	10·9	11·7	12·4	12·9	13·4	13·8	14·2	14·6
66	20	11·1	12·0	12·6	13·1	13·6	14·1	14·5	14·8
72	22	11·6	12·4	13·0	13·6	14·1	14·5	14·9	15·3
79	24	12·0	12·8	13·5	14·0	14·5	14·9	15·3	15·7
85	26	12·4	13·2	13·9	14·4	14·9	15·3	15·7	16·1
92	28	12·8	13·6	14·3	14·8	15·3	15·7	16·1	16·5

THE RUNNING FIX. The previous notes have described how a yacht's position can be fixed by making two observations at almost the same time. It will frequently be found however, when a fix is wanted, that only one suitable landmark is visible, and a bearing of this will only give one position line. Although a fix cannot be obtained at the time, the bearing should be taken, and the position line laid off on the chart, because often this position.line can be transferred and crossed with a second bearing taken later on of the same, or some other landmark. A fix obtained in this way is known as a running fix. Its accuracy will mainly depend upon the accuracy of the estimated track and distance made good between the bearings and therefore this should be as short as possible, consistent with the requirement that the angle of cut should be as large as possible.

The method to be used in order to obtain a running fix can best be shown by means of an example.

Example. At 2145, the lighthouse L bore 320° M. from a yacht steering 260° M. The log reading was 24. Later, at 2230, log reading 27, the same lighthouse bore 040° M. From the chart, the tidal stream was estimated to be setting 230° T. at 2 knots. Variation 10° W.

Find the yacht's position at 2230.

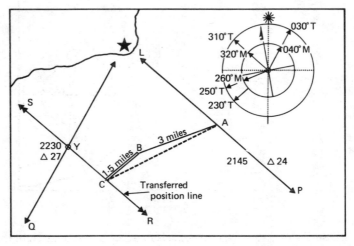

Fig. 7.11

Lay off the position lines PL and QL obtained from the bearings taken at 2145 and 2230 respectively. From any point A on the first position line, lay off the course made good through the water (allowing for leeway, if any) and the distance logged (AB = 3 miles) in the 45 minutes between the bearings. From B, lay off BC, which is the direction and distance (1.5 miles) the yacht is estimated to have been set by the tidal stream in 45 minutes. Then AC represents the estimated direction and distance made good over the ground between the bearings. Through C draw the line SYCR parallel to the first position line. The yacht's estimated position, 45 minutes after taking the first bearing, must lie somewhere on this line, which is known as a transferred position line, and is usually distinguished by two arrowheads at each end. The point Y, where the transferred position line cuts the second position line QL, is the yacht's position at 2230 (Fig. 7.11).

THE USE OF A SINGLE POSITION LINE. At times, when coasting or making the land in moderate visibility, it is only possible to obtain one position line. When this line lies in a suitable direction, it may often be used to clear some danger or to make the entrance to a harbour.

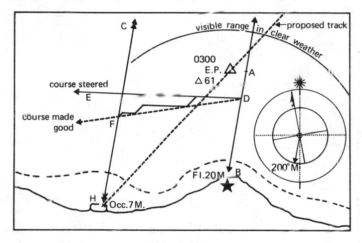

Fig. 7.12

Suppose, for example, that a yacht is making for harbour H, in the above figure, and is approaching the coast in moderate and decreasing visibility after a passage of about 50 miles since the last fix. Assume that at 0300, log reading 61, the powerful flashing light B is sighted bearing 200° M., obviously well within its maximum range, and that this bearing when drawn on the chart gives a position line which lies some miles to the eastward of the yacht's estimated position.

Although the yacht's most likely position on the position line is the point marked A nearest to her estimated position, her navigator cannot be sure of his distance from the light. Because of this and the decreasing visibility, he cannot safely alter course from A direct for the harbour, and assume that he will get a second bearing and hence a running fix, as he may not see the light again.

His safest plan, in these circumstances, is to assume that he is closer to the light than he thinks he is, for example at point D, and then to alter to a course (DE) which, bearing in mind the possible effect of the tidal stream, takes the yacht parallel to or, if necessary, away from the coast. He should then transfer his position line (HC) through the harbour entrance, or fairway buoy, and carefully plot his estimated position at intervals as he steers his new course. As soon as he estimates that he has reached the transferred position line (i.e. at F), he should alter course again, and steer a course that makes good the direction of the position line (i.e. 200° M.), counteracting the tidal stream as necessary. (Fig. 7.12).

He can then approach the harbour in reasonable safety, knowing the direction in which it lies, until the occulting light at the entrance is seen. If the visibility is poor during the final approach, occasional soundings should be taken, and if the light has not been seen by the time the soundings have decreased to say 6 fathoms in this example, the yacht should be turned about onto the opposite course, or anchored, until the visibility has improved. The limiting sounding must be governed by the nature of the particular coastline; for steep, rocky coastlines, the 20 metre (10 fathoms) line should be the limit, for shelving coastlines, the 10 metre (6 fathoms) line.

LINE OF SOUNDINGS. It is sometimes necessary to make a landfall and an approach to a position in conditions of poor visibility or fog. If possible some thought should be given to this and preparations made to assist in making the approach safely, so that the yacht's position is known with reasonable certainty. Assuming that radar is not carried and that radio direction finding is not usable in the particular area concerned, it will mean that soundings (preferably with an echo sounder) and fog signals will have to be used. If the approach is to be made to a position off a lighthouse which operates a fog signal, or to a harbour entrance, the destination position must be chosen so that there is a reasonable chance of hearing the fog signal. The position must not be too far from the lighthouse. At the same time, it must be possible to check whether a wrong approach is being made, by sounding, in case the fog signal is not heard. Remember sound signals in fog are notoriously uncertain (see page 17), but may be all that is available. Some limit must be put on the approach, either distance run, or minimum

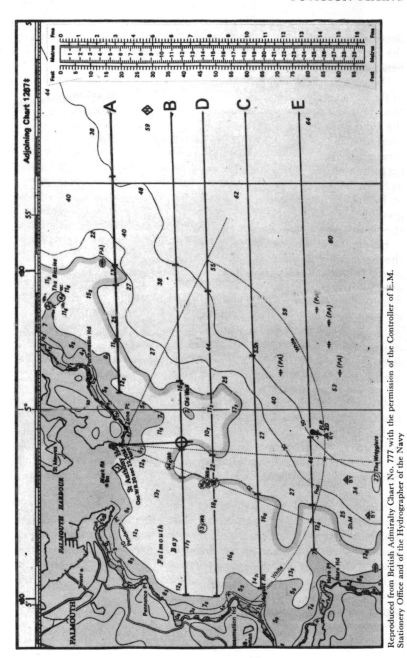

Fig. 7.13

Reproduced from British Admiralty Chart No. 777 with the permission of the Controller of H.M.
Stationery Office and of the Hydrographer of the Navy

sounding, so that if the position is not made and positively identified, the boat can be anchored, stopped or turned round, to await improved visibility.

An example may help to show how a line of soundings may be used to decide a yacht's position in thick fog. It must be borne in mind that in any such approach, some allowance must be made for the height of tide, if soundings are to be used to fix the yacht's position. Before a sounding is compared with the soundings on the chart, the approximate height of tide must be subtracted to "reduce" the sounding to chart datum. This process is known as "Reduction to soundings".

In the example which is considered now, of a yacht making for a position one mile south of St. Anthony Head in the approaches to Falmouth in thick fog, having started from a position two miles south of Eddystone lighthouse some 27 miles to the eastward, there would probably have been sufficient time to have estimated the height of tide in the Falmouth approaches using the method shown on page 39. In this illustration, for example, if the approach had been made on the afternoon of 26 August 1973, B.S.T., the height of tide would have been approximately 3 metres at 1400, 4 metres at 1500, 4.7 metres at 1600 and 5 metres at H.W. around 1700. (Based on H.W. Falmouth at 1704 B.S.T. height 5.1 metres, duration of rise 6h.05m., and Mean Level 2.9 metres). This would mean, if the yacht was crossing the 50 metre contour line on the chart at about 1500, that the actual sounding when this occurred would be 54 metres ($29\frac{1}{2}$ fathoms), and the time should be noted when 54 metres ($29\frac{1}{2}$ fathoms) is observed on the sounder. (Fig. 7.13).

It is assumed that the approach is being made on auxiliary engine at 3 knots over the ground and steering to make good a course of 268° T. whilst listening for the fog signal which is a Horn. In this discussion the 30 metre line has been disregarded to avoid complication.

If the attempted approach line is B, and soundings are observed, the following might be the possible pattern of corrected soundings and times recorded along the different marked approach lines shown in Fig. 7.13. Time intervals are in minutes between the respective contour lines. (Fig. 7.14).

The 10 metre line has been taken as the absolute limit line to turn on or anchor.

If A was the approach line, the fog signal may not be heard because of the land intervening, but if heard, it should appear to come from ahead. The 5 minute interval when the soundings de-

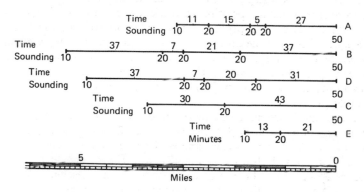

Fig. 7.14

creased from 20m. and then increased again to 20m. is fairly distinctive. Decisions may have to be made fairly early in an approach such as this. If the dividers are set to the distance observed between say the 50m. and 20m. contour, i.e. 27 mins, at 3 knots is 1.4 miles, and are then moved over the chart parallel to the track, it may be possible to estimate the probable track after one line has been crossed. A better indication may be given after a further line has been timed. The lines shown above show that in this area, each line of soundings is probably unique, and could be used to fit to the chart to obtain a line of position.

If B was being made good, it is possible the horn fog signal would be heard apparently about 45° on the starboard bow as the 20m. line was approached. If so the signal would gradually broaden on the bow, until when the 20m. line is crossed again, it would be heard apparently on the starboard beam after about 21 minutes. The pattern for D is very similar as it is only half a mile south of B.

If the yacht had been set to the south, on tracks C or E, the soundings would decrease continuously in a fairly distinctive way, but the fog signal might not be heard.

The situation might develop as follows, with the soundings indicating that the yacht is probably making good track D, it could be envisaged, having heard the fog signal gradually broaden on the starboard bow until it is at last apparently abeam, with sounding at 20m. for the second time, that course could be altered to about 345° T. to put the fog signal a few degrees on the starboard bow again, so that a closer approach could be made in order to sight the lighthouse if possible. If nothing is sighted by the time the 10m. contour is reached, the yacht should be anchored to await improved visibility. If the yacht is apparently to the southward on tracks C or E, on reaching the 10m. line it should be either stopped or anchored. From there it may be possible to follow the 10m. line to the north until something is sighted and identified, or the yacht is anchored closer to the entrance in 10 metres. If there are doubts at any time, stop, anchor if possible, or turn and re-trace the track for a bit.

Reproduced from British Admiralty Instructional Chart No. 5066 with the permission of the Controller of H.M. Stationery Office and of the Hydrographer of the Navy

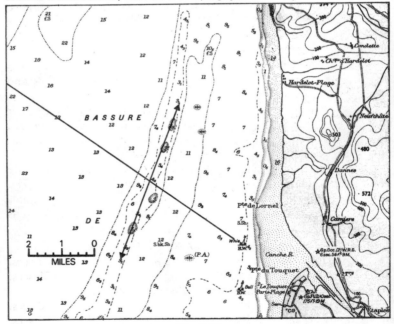

Fig. 7.15

A more positive position line is obtained by taking a line of soundings when the yacht crosses a clearly defined shallow ridge or deeper slot in the seabed as shown in the figure of the approaches to Le Touquet (Fig. 7.15). This should not be done in a blow, as there may be heavy breaking seas. The crossing of the ridge enclosed by the 6 fathom line (– – – – – –) with soundings of 3 to 4 fathoms gives a clear position line with an accuracy of about 4 cables. The later crossing, about one mile further on, of the 10 fathom line (· — · — · — · — · — ·) again is a clear position line giving an indication of how many miles to go in poor visibility. It might be used in conjunction with the lighthouse or light in moderate visibility to fix position.

The pattern of soundings has got to be suitable for a line of soundings to be used in this way, and generally the contour lines should be continuous, with no areas marked with no soundings, which would indicate a poor and incomplete survey.

Radio Aids to Navigation

RADIOBEACONS. Marine radiobeacons are generally radio transmitters which transmit easily identifiable signals in all directions, so that a vessel fitted with direction finding apparatus can fix its position in fog, or when other suitable landmarks are too far off to be visible.

The abbreviation Ro. Bn. in black, or RC in magenta, plus a magenta circle in each case, indicate on charts the lighthouses and lightvessels equipped with radiobeacons.

Many beacons provide a continuous service by transmitting their characteristic signals for one minute at regular specified intervals, day and night, in fog and in clear weather; other beacons transmit only in fog, and make no clear weather transmissions.

All marine radiobeacons situated on the coasts of Europe and the British Isles transmit on frequencies between 285 and 315 kHz. (1053 and 952 metres), and the form of the characteristic signals transmitted by those north of Lat. 46° N., has been standardised as follows:

1. The identification signal transmitted 3 to 6 times
   for approx.   22 secs.
2. A long dash lasting for   25 secs.
3. The identification signal transmitted once or twice
   for approx.   8 secs.
4. A silent period of at least   5 secs.
                                                               _____
                                              Total   60 secs.
                                                               _____

A prolonged silent period usually follows. A beacon's identification signal usually consists of two letters transmitted in the morse code.

In order to make it easier to obtain a fix in certain areas, certain beacons have been linked in groups. Each group consists of 2, 3, or 6 beacons which transmit one at a time on the same frequency. This allows at least two bearings of different beacons to be obtained without retuning the receiver.

Certain aircraft radiobeacons are situated near the coast, and these may often be used to obtain bearings when other beacons are not suitable. They should, however, be used with caution because of possible coastal refraction (see later note). Their characteristic signals usually consist of a two or three letter identification signal in morse, followed by a long dash, and they usually operate continuously between stated times.

The ranges, signals, frequencies and transmission times of beacons in European waters are contained in the Admiralty List of Radio Signals, Vol. II. and Reed's Nautical Almanac.

THE PRINCIPLE OF THE DIRECTION FINDER is based upon the directive properties of a plane vertical loop aerial, or alternatively a horizontal ferrite rod aerial. The strength of the signal heard in the earphones depends upon the angle between the vertical plane through the aerial and the direction of the beacon. As the aerial is slowly rotated, so the signal strength varies from a maximum to zero. The rate of change of signal strength is greatest near the zero positions, and therefore the bearing pointer is fixed to the aerial so that the direction of the incoming radio waves is indicated when the signal strength is zero. This occurs when the plane of a loop aerial is at right angles to, or when a rod aerial is in line with, the direction of the beacon respectively. Two zero positions, approximately 180° apart, will be observed if the rod or loop is rotated through 360°, and therefore an approximate bearing of each beacon must be obtained from the yacht's estimated position on the chart in order to decide which one is correct.

The zero position is either obtained aurally by using the earphones, or visually by means of a signal strength meter. A sense-finding circuit is included in some receivers and this can be used to resolve the 180° ambiguity mentioned above, by following the makers' instructions.

PROCEDURE. Bearings obtained with the fixed type of set are relative to the boat's fore and aft line. These are expressed in three figures where 000° indicates ahead, 090° indicates the starboard beam, 180° indicates astern, and 270° indicates the port beam, as shown in Fig. 7.16. This type of set should be fixed if possible in line

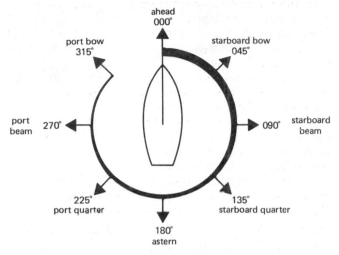

port bow
315°

ahead
000°

starboard bow
045°

port
beam   270°

090°   starboard
beam

225°
port quarter

135°
starboard quarter

180°
astern

RELATIVE BEARINGS

Fig. 7.16

with the keel and as far away from the mast and rigging as possible.
The 0° – 180° line on the bearing plate should be in, or parallel to,
the boat's fore and aft line. In steel yachts bearings will have to be
taken from a position on deck.

After the yacht's estimated position has been marked on a small
scale chart, the 2 (3 if possible) nearest beacons which will give a
reasonable angle of cut should be chosen, and their approximate
bearings relative to the yacht's course, obtained from the chart.
The frequencies, identification signals and times of transmission
are then obtained from one of the publications previously mentioned, and the set tuned to the frequency of the first beacon to transmit.
If the beacons chosen are grouped, the set will not require retuning.
Each bearing is taken in the following manner, after disconnecting
the vertical aerial (if any) and plugging in the earphones.

The loop or rod is rotated until the bearing pointer is roughly at
right angles to the beacon's direction obtained from the chart so
that, as soon as the beacon transmits, its signal will be heard at
maximum strength.

After the beacon has been heard and identified, and as soon as the
long continuous note commences, the loop or rod should be rotated
until the signal is no longer heard. The aerial should then be swung
slightly each side of this direction in order to decide the exact zero

POSITION FIXING

position. As soon as this is achieved the bearing and the exact compass heading of the boat should be noted at the same instant, together with the time and log reading. The bearings for the chart are then obtained by adding the corrected D.F. bearings (see later note on quadrantal error) to the boat's true or magnetic heading, subtracting 360° if necessary, to produce true or magnetic bearings respectively.

The fixed type of D.F. set will be probably used in larger yachts or fishing vessels. It has been largely superseded in small yachts by the hand held instrument which incorporates a ferrite rod aerial and a bearing compass and is shown in Fig. 4.9B/C.

When taking bearings with this type, the receiver and rod aerial must be tuned to the frequency of the beacon, which must be identified with the rod aerial approximately at right angles to the direction of the beacon (i.e. the maximum signal position). On hearing the long dash, the instrument must be rotated until the signal is zero and then oscillated slightly each side of this position until it is clearly identified. The bearing is then read from vertically above the card, or by facing the direction of the beacon and viewing the bearing in the prism. Bearings obtained in this way may have to be corrected for quadrantal error and for compass deviation before plotting them on the chart. Errors due to yawing of the boat should be reduced by using this type of instrument. Where the aerial, compass and the receiver are in one unit, the batteries should be checked before fitting to see if they cause any compass deviation. They may require de-magnetising.

Example. The following D.F. bearings were obtained when approaching the French coast, using fixed D.F. equipment:

At 1303, Roches Douvres radiobeacon bore 296° relative, quadrantal error −1°, with the yacht heading 169° C. At 1304, Ile de Batz radiobeacon bore 048° relative, quadrantal error +4°, with the yacht heading 172° C. Deviation 1° W. (*High*), variation 8° W. (*High*), log reading 73. What are the true bearings to lay off on the chart? (Fig. 7.17).

Roches Douvres				*Ile de Batz*			
Comp. Co.	169°C.	D.F. brg.	296°	Comp. Co.	172°C.	D.F. brg.	048°
Dev.	−1°H.	Quad. err.	−1°	Dev.	−1°H.	Quad. err.	+4°
Mag. Co.	168°M.	Rel. brg.	295°	Mag. Co.	171°M.	Rel. brg.	052°
Var.	−8°H.	True Co.	+160°T.	Var.	−8°H.	True Co.	+163°T.
True Co.	160°T.		455°	True Co.	163°T.	True brg.	215°T.
			−360°				
		True Brg.	095°T.				

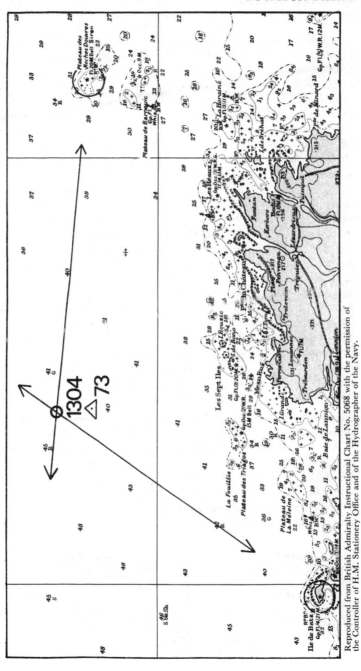

Fig. 7.17

Reproduced from British Admiralty Instructional Chart No. 5068 with the permission of the Controller of H.M. Stationery Office and of the Hydrographer of the Navy.

If the bearings had been taken on the above yacht using a hand held D.F. instrument, assumed to be unaffected by compass deviation, the observations might have been recorded as under:

At 1303 with course approximately 170° C., deviation 1° W. (*High*), Roches Douvres radiobeacon bore 104° M., and at 1304 Ile de Batz radiobeacon bore 219° M. Variation 8° W. (*High*). What are the true bearings if the quadrantal error curve shows −1° and +4° for relative bearings of 295° Rel. and 050° Rel?

Compass Co. 170° C. −1° W. (*High*) = <u>Magnetic Co. 169° M.</u>

Roches Douvres					Ile de Batz			
Mag. brg.	104°M.	D.F. Mag. brg.	104°M.		Mag. brg.	219°M.	D.F. Mag. brg.	219°M.
	+360°	Quad. err.	−1°		Mag. Co.	−169°M.	Quad. err.	+4°
	464°	Mag. brg.	103°M.		Rel. brg. for			
Mag. Co.	−169°M.	Var.	−8°H.		Quad. err.	050°	Mag. brg.	223°M.
Rel. brg. for					Quad. err.	+4°	Var.	−8°H.
Quad. err.	295°	True brg.	095°T.				True brg.	215°T.
Quad. err.	−1°							

Note: If there is no quadrantal error curve, there is no need to work out the relative bearing for each observation. The variation is applied to the bearing to get the true bearing. This is quicker and easier, but might be less accurate.

If a small "cocked hat" results from bearings of three well placed beacons, considerable reliance may be placed on the fix. If the cocked hat is large, the observations should be repeated if possible; if this is not possible, the fix should be regarded as unreliable. Practice D.F. bearings should be taken whenever possible, particularly when the resulting fixes can be checked by visual bearings, as a navigator can thereby judge the accuracy of his radio bearings. This will help him to decide how much reliance he can place on a fix when only radio bearings are available. D.F. bearings are not the be all and end all of navigation because they are quite difficult to take accurately and are subject to errors. They should be regarded as aids to navigation to be used with all the other information available.

Errors

NIGHT EFFECT. During the period from one hour before sunset to one hour after sunrise, signals from beacons situated more than 25 miles from the vessel, may be received via the ionosphere (sky waves) as well as parallel to the earth's surface (ground waves). The reception of sky waves may cause the signals to fade, or give blurred and indefinite zeros, and bearings which are obtained by using such signals are liable to be incorrect. During the above period therefore, D.F. bearings should only be taken of beacons which are less than 25 miles from the vessel.

COASTAL REFRACTION (LAND EFFECT). Ground waves from a beacon situated some distance inland may be deflected towards the coastline by as much as 5° if they cross the coast at an oblique angle as they pass from land to sea. Waves travelling parallel to a coastline may be deflected either away from it, or towards it. When this occurs, the bearing obtained will not indicate the direction of the beacon. To avoid this error, always use marine beacons if possible, and if an aircraft beacon has to be used, choose one where the path of the wave from beacon to vessel crosses the coastline nearly at right angles.

QUADRANTAL ERROR. This error is caused by the vessel's hull, rigging and mast, which sometimes deflect radio waves so that incorrect bearings are obtained. If possible, the lower ends of shrouds and stays should be insulated from their rigging screws and chain plates. Plastic tubing or a good marline service over the wire where it passes round the thimble is satisfactory. If this is carried out, errors in wooden vessels will probably be negligible, but in steel vessels may still be appreciable.

In order to detect these errors, D.F. and visual relative bearings should be obtained at intervals of 10° or 20° all round the vessel, by steadying her on many different courses when she is 3 to 5 miles from a radiobeacon. At least two people will be required, one to

Table 7.3

A	B	C	D	E	F	G
Ship's Head by Steering Compass	Steering Compass Deviation (if any)	Magnetic Heading (A+B)	Magnetic Bearing of Beacon by Hand Bearing Compass	Relative Bearing (D − C)	D.F. Bearing (Relative)	Error (E − F)
080°C	5° LOW	085° M	128° M	043°	039°	+4°
062°C	5° LOW	067° M	132° M	065°	062°	+3°
052°C	5° LOW	057° M	140° M	083°	081°	+2°

and so on

take the D.F. bearings, and the other to steer the vessel, note the ship's head and take bearings with the hand bearing compass as the D.F. bearings are taken. Table 7.3 will give some idea of what is required.

The vessel is steadied on a suitable course, and then one person takes a D.F. bearing of the beacon (column F.) The other person immediately notes the ship's head (column A), then takes and notes the bearing of the beacon with the hand bearing compass (column D). This procedure is carried out on a succession of courses so that the relative bearing changes by about 20° between each bearing. The remaining columns are completed after all the bearings have been taken. Column E is completed by subtracting C from D, after adding 360° to D if necessary. The errors are obtained by subtracting F from E. If the bearing in F is greater than that in E, the error is negative. Note that the sign of the error indicates how it should be applied to a D.F. bearing in order to obtain the correct relative bearing.

If the hand held type of D.F. instrument is checked for quadrantal error, the columns in the table should be drawn up as under after one person has noted the boat's head by compass, and the other has taken the D.F. bearing and then the visual bearing with the same instrument. (Table 7.4).

Table 7.4

A	B	C	D	E	F	G
Boat's Head by Steering Compass	Steering Compass Deviation (if any)	Magnetic Heading (A ± B)	Visual Magnetic Bearing of Beacon by hand bearing compass	D.F. Magnetic Bearing of Beacon by hand held instrument	Relative D.F. Bearing (E − C)	Error (D − E)
080°C	5° LOW	085°M	128° M	124° M	039°	+ 4°

and so on

It is assumed in columns D and E that the compass used has no deviation at the positions from which the bearings were taken. The errors should either be tabulated against D.F. bearings, or a curve drawn with plus errors marked above, and minus errors marked below, a horizontal axis indicating D.F. bearings and marked from 0° to 360°.

CONSOL. Consol is a long range navigational aid primarily intended for the use of aircraft. It can be used by vessels equipped with a suitable medium frequency receiver. Consol signals can be received on any of the sets designed and sold for use in yachts.

A Consol beacon consists of an automatic radio transmitter with a special directional aerial system. The radiation pattern from each beacon consists of alternate sectors of dot and dash signals, separated by equisignals. (An equisignal is heard faintly as a short, steady note). Each sector is approximately 15° wide, and the radiation pattern on one side of the line of the aerials is the mirror image of the pattern on the other side (see Fig. 7.18). During each transmission cycle, the two halves of the pattern rotate uniformly in opposite directions until each equisignal has moved through one sector's width. The rotation then ceases and the pattern reverts to its original position ready for the next cycle. During this short time the beacon's identification signal (2 or 3 letters in morse) and a long dash are transmitted. An observer will therefore hear an equisignal once in each cycle, and his angular position in a sector is determined by the number of dot or dash characters heard before the equisignal.

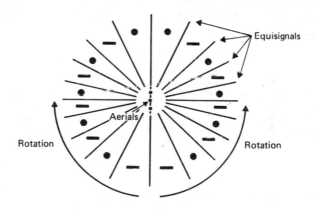

Fig. 7.18   Radiation Pattern of Consol Beacon

METHOD OF USE. Tune the receiver to the frequency of the beacon, and correctly identify it by listening for the identification signal. Where possible a vertical aerial should be used, but a D.F. set may be used as long as the loop is not turned away more than 45° either side of its position for maximum signal strength. The total number of dots and dashes heard is then counted by the observer.

If he is in a dot sector he will hear dots, equisignal and then dashes; in a dash sector he will hear dashes, equisignal and then dots. The total number of dots and dashes heard should add up to 60, but in practice some of the characters are lost because they appear to merge in the equisignal at the change from one symbol to the other. The actual count is therefore corrected to allow for the lost characters by subtracting the total observed count from 60, and adding half the difference to the dot count, and half to the dash count.

For example: Observed count 40 dashes – equisignal – 16 dots.
Total count 56. Difference 60 – 56 = 4. Half diff. =2.
Corrected count 42 dashes – equisignal – 18 dots.

A position line is obtained by applying the average of several counts of the characters heard *before* the equisignal to a Consol chart, which has position lines printed on it at 5 or 10 character intervals. The position lines appropriate to each beacon are marked in different colours.

A corrected count will give a position line in each of several sectors, so that the vessel's estimated position must be plotted on the Consol chart to decide which is the correct sector. The exact position line can then be easily interpolated by eye in the vicinity of the estimated position.

The vessel's position can be fixed by taking a count on a second Consol beacon, and thus obtaining a second position line.

COVERAGE is about 140° on either side of the aerial base line at each of 4 beacons. These are situated at Stavanger (Norway), Bushmills (N. Ireland), Plonéis (N. W. France), and Lugo (Spain).

The system can therefore be used in all waters surrounding the coast of N. W. Europe and the British Isles. A position line cannot be obtained from a beacon when the vessel is within 25 miles of it.

ACCURACY. The system is not considered sufficiently accurate for making a landfall, or when closing danger, but is a useful aid in more open waters.

Example. Whilst on passage from Portsmouth to Le Havre, the following Consol counts were obtained:

Bushmills   3 dashes   –   equisignal   –   51 dots
Plonéis   25 dots   –   equisignal   –   31 dashes

The yacht's estimated position was Lat. 50° 08′ N. Long. 0° 34′ W. Required to fix the yacht's position.

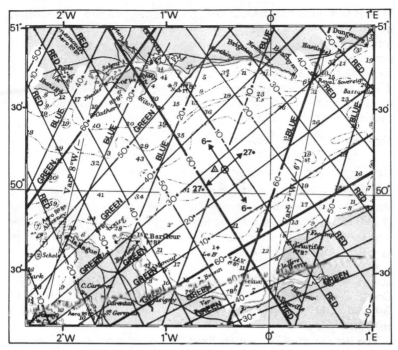

Reproduced from British Admiralty Chart No. L2 Consol with the permission of the Controller of H.M. Stationery Office and of the Hydrographer of the Navy

Fig.7.19   A Consol Fix

The corrected counts are:

Bushmills   6 dashes   –   equisignal   –   54 dots
Ploneis   27 dots   –   equisignal   –   33 dashes

The 6 dash position line for Bushmills, and the 27 dot position line for Ploneis are marked in Fig. 7.19. The yacht's position was Lat. 50° 08′ N., Long 0° 28′ W.

Chapter 8

Passage Making

PLANNING A PASSAGE. The charts and "pilots" required for the passage should be obtained some time before the proposed departure day, so that they can be studied at leisure and a plan prepared before sailing. These should include charts for harbours and coasts which lie near the waters in which the passage is to be made in case the plan has to be altered because of bad weather or other causes.

The track to be followed should be drawn on a small scale chart which shows both the point of departure and the destination. It can then be redrawn on the large scale charts which will be used while making the passage.

The track should be drawn close enough to the shore to make certain that all lighthouses and beacons can be seen so that frequent fixes can be obtained. As a guide, when the coast is steep – to aim to pass it at a distance of about 2 miles; when the coast is shelving, yachts drawing less than 3 metres (10 feet) should pass outside the 5 metre (3 fathom) line. Areas where overfalls or races are experienced should be avoided. Where there are unmarked dangers out of sight of land, aim to pass them at a distance of at least 5 miles, and if they are to be passed at night, this distance should be increased.

Departure should be timed to give the longest possible period with a fair tidal stream during the passage. The most suitable time can be worked out by marking each page in the tidal stream atlas with the actual times appropriate for the chosen day of sailing and the following day, and then from various assumed starting times running through the passage at the boat's estimated speed, increasing or decreasing it as necessary to allow for the probable tidal stream effect. When considering departure times, other factors which may decide the best time should be borne in mind. For instance, it may be necessary to arrive at a certain position at slack water, or at a harbour entrance at daybreak; after a passage partly out of sight of land, it is often easier to make a landfall just before dawn when lights are still visible. In these cases, it is better to work back from the required position and time in order to find the departure time. When finally deciding a suitable time, some allowance should always be made for unforeseen wind shifts etc., and for the fact that a vessel nearly always tends to be late at a position rather than early.

Finally, before sailing, a weather forecast should be obtained through one of the B.B.C. broadcasts, or by telephone to one of the Meteorological Offices. Full details of the times of broadcast weather forecasts and other services, are contained in Reed's Nautical Almanac.

Yachtsmen making a coastal passage in UK waters are strongly advised to contact the local H.M. Coastguard station to complete a Coastguard CG 66 Passage report form. This ensures that the Coastguard service has full particulars regarding the craft, occupants, its equipment and intended voyage, for use should search and rescue action be needed. At his destination, the yachtsman must report his arrival, by telephone is sufficient, to the nearest Coastguard station. If weather or other circumstances have necessitated a change of plan so that the boat arrives at a different place to that intended, this arrival must be reported. There is no charge for this service.

MAKING A PASSAGE. After leaving her berth, a yacht will usually have to be navigated by buoys, beacons, or leads until she reaches the sea. This should not present any difficulty in clear weather if the chart has been studied before leaving. When leaving (or entering) harbours with narrow entrances, a careful watch should be kept for harbour traffic signals, which are displayed to stop vessels leaving when a vessel is entering, or vice versa.

Such signals are described in the "Pilot" for the area and many are given in Reed's Nautical Almanac. They must be obeyed. After passing the harbour or river entrance, it may still be necessary to navigate for some miles along one of a number of different channels between sandbanks before the departure point for the passage is reached (e.g. Thames Estuary). In these circumstances, the name or number of each buoy to be passed, together with the magnetic or compass course from each buoy to the next, should be written in a notebook so that it can be referred to whenever the direction of the next buoy is not known with certainty. This would be of great assistance in poor visibility and near areas where two or more channels combine, as it is very easy to steer for the wrong buoy unless this precaution is taken. On a rising tide sandbanks may often be crossed with safety in fine weather after the tide has risen sufficiently to give a good clearance under the keel, but no risk should be taken on a falling tide as if the yacht grounds she would be unlikely to refloat for several hours.

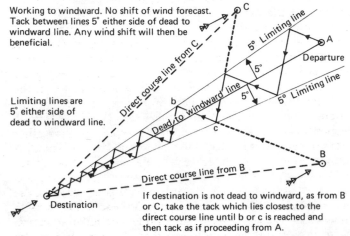

Working to windward. No shift of wind forecast. Tack between lines 5° either side of dead to windward line. Any wind shift will then be beneficial.

Limiting lines are 5° either side of dead to windward line.

If destination is not dead to windward, as from B or C, take the tack which lies closest to the direct course line until b or c is reached and then tack as if proceeding from A.

Fig. 8.1

The log should be streamed or switched on before reaching the end of the approach channel, and as soon as the last buoy is passed, the yacht should be put on her first course, counteracting the tidal stream if necessary. The log should then be set to zero, or its reading noted, and together with the time, written on the chart alongside the buoy. Her position should then be fixed at regular intervals by cross bearings while suitable landmarks are visible. When making a passage out of sight of land, the yacht's estimated position should be plotted at regular intervals as convenient. If a direction-finder is carried the estimated positions can occasionally be checked and adjusted by taking D.F. bearings.

A sailing yacht will often find that her destination or the position off the next headland, lies dead to windward, and she will then have to tack each side of her direct course. In these circumstances it will not pay her to deviate too far from the direct course line, unless a shift of wind is forecast, or perhaps a favourable tidal stream or smoother water will be experienced. A good plan is to keep her tacking within two lines drawn about 5° on either side of the direct course line as shown in Fig. 8.1. If a shift of wind is forecast these two lines should be drawn on the same side of the direct course line as the wind is expected to shift, (see Fig. 8.2). If a tidal stream has also to be considered when working to windward, a yacht should be kept for as long as possible on the tack that makes the least angle with the direction of a foul tidal stream; on the other hand she should be kept on the tack that makes the largest angle with the direction of a fair tidal stream.

If fog or mist sets in during a passage, lifejackets should be put on and a fog signal made at intervals of not more than one minute, preferably with a fog-horn. If the practice of regularly fixing the yacht's position has been followed, there will be a recent fix on the chart, which can be used to estimate her present position and decide future action. A yacht situated in a busy shipping lane is in a dangerous position, as small craft are not easily detected on other vessel's radar screens, and her fog signal is usually low powered. A yacht may sometimes be detected on a radar screen at a greater range if a metal radar reflector is hoisted to the masthead, but this should not be relied upon to indicate the yacht's presence, because radar is not carried by all vessels. Probably the best action to take, is to work her clear of the shipping lane into less frequented waters. If the coast is near and shelving, she can then stand in towards the shore, taking frequent soundings, until the water is shallow enough to anchor; off a rocky steep coastline, she should be kept well clear of the shore.

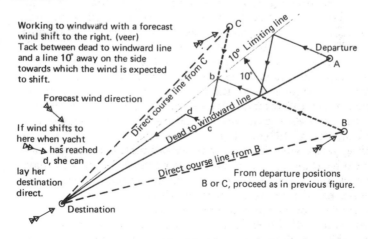

Working to windward with a forecast wind shift to the right. (veer)
Tack between dead to windward line and a line 10° away on the side towards which the wind is expected to shift.

Forecast wind direction

If wind shifts to here when yacht has reached d, she can lay her destination direct.

Destination

C

10° Limiting line

Departure

A

Direct course line from C

b

10°

d

Dead to windward line

c

B

Direct course line from B

From departure positions B or C, proceed as in previous figure.

Fig. 8.2

119

If it is decided to continue the passage, the navigator will have to make use of all the aids at his disposal to keep a check on his yacht's position. These include a good lookout, soundings, air fog signals from lighthouses, lightvessels and buoys, and D.F. bearings when a suitable set is carried. He must also carefully plot his estimated position at regular intervals. Many lighthouses and lightvessels indicate their positions by making characteristic air fog signals at regular intervals. The chart abbreviations and descriptions of the signals are given on page 18.

These fog signals are heard at greatly varying distances, and on occasions they may be inaudible, even when close to the station, because of the prevailing air conditions. They must always be approached with caution, and other means of finding the yacht's position must not be neglected.

When navigating along a coast from fog signal to fog signal, the course steered should allow for any tidal stream effect so that she makes good a track which lies roughly parallel to the coastline and passes close enough to the fog signal for it to be heard. Check soundings should be taken, and sometimes where the charted soundings are closely spaced and regular, a contour line may be followed until the fog signal is heard.

If the yacht is coming in from the sea to try to hear a fog signal, it is not normally advisable to steer straight for it. Her navigator should steer for a point on a suitable contour line several miles to one side of the fog signal, so that when his soundings tell him that he has reached this contour line, he will know with some certainty on which side of his yacht the fog signal lies. He can then alter course parallel to the coast, and follow the contour line towards the fog signal.

ARRIVING AT THE DESTINATION. The "Pilot" should be read and the chart examined before entering so that the navigator has a "picture" of the place in his mind. If the destination is an anchorage, the height of tide must be known so that the yacht can be anchored in sufficient depth of water to ensure that she remains afloat at low water. The "Pilot" will usually describe suitable anchorages, and the best approach to them. As soon as the yacht is anchored, the depth of water should be checked with the lead, and anchor bearings taken. These can be used to check whether the yacht is dragging if the wind increases.

Index

Abbreviations, 6–7
Allowing for streams, 80–82
Arriving, 120

Bearings, 65, 76–77
  D. F. 106–110
Boat's head, 65
Boat's lead, 58–59
Buoyage, 18–28

Cable, 2
Calibrating, D. F., 111–112
Charts, 3–4
Chart datum, 31, 39–40
Chart table, 48
Cocked hat, 87
Compass cards, 50–51
Compass course, 72–75
Compass errors, 65
Compass rose, 72, 73
Consol, 113–115
Contour lines, 105, 41
Course, 65
  correction, 72

Dead reckoning position, 83
Deviation, 68
  curve, 69, 71
  table, 70
Dipping distance, 94
Direction finding, D. F., 62–63,
  106–112
Distance, 2–4
Distance of sea horizon, 94, 96
Dividers, 49
Drying heights, 40
Duration of mean rise, 35
Dutchman's log, 58

Echo sounder, principle, 59–60
  types, 59–62
Estimating position, 83–84

Fathom, 2
Fixing position, 84–115
Flood stream, 20–21
Fog, 119–120
Fog signals, 17–18

Geographical range, 13, 94, 96–97
Grid compass, 53–54

Hand bearing compass, 52, 54
Harbour signals, 117
Height differences, 33–35
Height of tide, 38–39
High water, 29–30
Horizontal angles, 87, 89–91

Knot, 2

Lanby, 16
Land effect, 111
L.A.T. See Lowest Astronomical
  Tide
Latitude, 1
Leads, 14
Leeway, 78–79
Lights, 9–15
Lightvessels, 16
Logs, 55–58
Longitude, 1
Lowest Astronomical Tide, 31
Luminous range, 13

INDEX

Magnetic Compass, 50
Magnetic course, 73–76
Making a passage, 117–120
Mean High Water Springs, 34, 35
Mean Level, 35
Metre, 2
Metric charts, 5–6
MHWS *See* Mean High Water
  Springs

Neaps, 30
Night effect, 110—111
Nominal range, 97
Notices to Mariners, 7–8

Parallel rulers, 48–49
Patent log, 55
Perches, 28
Planning a passage, 116–117
Plotting, 83–84
Points, 51
Position lines, 84–86, 98, 99

Quality of bottom, 41
Quadrantal error, 111–112

Radar reflectors, 19, 119
Radiobeacons, 105–106
Radio receivers, 62–64
Range of lights, 94–96
  of tides, 29
Reduction to soundings, 102
Relative bearings, 106–107
Rising distance, 94

Rule of twelfths, 39
Running fix, 97–99

Scale, 3
Secondary ports, 31
Second trace echoes, 61–62
Shallow water effects, 37–38
Single position line, 99–100
Soundings, 39–40
  line of, 100–105
Springs, 30
Standard ports, 31
Steering compasses, 51, 52, 53
Swing for deviation, 68–72
Symbols, 6–7

Tides, 29–40
Tidal streams, 42–44, 47, 79–80
  rates, 43–44
  tables, 43
Tide levels, 34
Time differences, 33–34
Transferred position line, 98, 99
Transit, 85, 86
True bearing, 76
True course, 72

Variation, 66–67

Weather forecasts, 117
Wind, 78–79
Windward work, 118, 119
Withies, 28